Advance Praise for How to Write & Give a Sp

"There should be a law against boring and poorly delivered speeches. When there is, Joan Detz will be required reading."
—Brian S. Akre, director of executive communications, Renault-Nissan BV

"If you want to boost your career, do two things: buy Joan Detz's book, then start giving great speeches."
—Jane Maas, author of *Mad Women* and advertising executive

"It's a rare distinction for any book to remain in print continuously for three decades. This thirtieth anniversary edition, updated for the digital age, attests to Joan Detz's international reputation as a corporate communicator par *excellence*. Her guidance goes far beyond speechwriting. The practical wisdom in these pages will help you communicate your best in every business situation."
—Marian Calabro, author of *The Clorox Company—100 Years, 1000 Reasons* and president, CorporateHistory.net

"Global executives need to give presentations. This book tells how to make those presentations effective."
—Olli-Pekka Kallasvuo, vice chairman, Telia-Sonera AB and SRV Group; former CEO, Nokia Corp.

"Full of terrific tips for researching, organizing, and delivering a speech."
—John Verrico, president-elect, National Association of Government Communicators

"A timeless reference manual."
—Carri Chandler, external affairs, Toyota Motor Engineering & Manufacturing North America, Inc.

"Joan Detz, with her vast experience and expertise, is certain to provide any communicator with great practical guidance and, more important, an added sense of purpose in what they do for a living."
—Vuk Vujnovic, secretary general at SEECOM (South East Europe Public Sector Communication Association)

"A broad range of new examples that illustrate the art and craft of speech-writing."
—Rhea Wessel, journalist and speechwriter

"Detz's book is a treasure trove of strategic and tactical speechwriting tips."
—Chris McGee, corporate speechwriter and former military public affairs specialist

"Joan's experience and expertise regarding speechwriting and presentation skills have proven to be invaluable."
—Vern Schellenger, SVP of HR, American Bankers Association

ALSO BY JOAN DETZ

Can You Say a Few Words?

It's Not What You Say, It's How You Say It

You Mean I Have to Stand Up and Say Something?

How to Write & Give a Speech

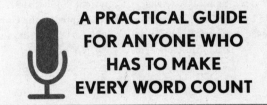

**A PRACTICAL GUIDE
FOR ANYONE WHO
HAS TO MAKE
EVERY WORD COUNT**

JOAN DETZ

St. Martin's Griffin
New York

HOW TO WRITE & GIVE A SPEECH. Copyright © 1984, 1992, 2002, 2014 by Joan Detz. All rights reserved. Printed in the United States of America. For information, address St. Martin's Press, 175 Fifth Avenue, New York, N.Y. 10010.

www.stmartins.com

The Library of Congress Cataloging-in-Publication Data is available upon request.

ISBN 978-1-250-04107-4 (trade paperback)
ISBN 978-1-4668-3722-5 (e-book)

St. Martin's Griffin books may be purchased for educational, business, or promotional use. For information on bulk purchases, please contact Macmillan Corporate and Premium Sales Department at 1-800-221-7945, extension 5442, or write specialmarkets@macmillan.com.

Third Revised Edition: March 2014

10   9   8   7   6   5   4   3   2   1

Dedicated to the writers who have attended
my speechwriting seminars since
I began the classes in 1992.
Choose excellence. Surpass yourself.
Plus ultra.

CONTENTS

ACKNOWLEDGMENTS

So many people helped during the process of writing this book. Thank you, all.

I particularly want to note: Brian Akre, Shell; Richard Batson, US Coast Guard; Sabra Brown, US Air Force; Carri Chandler, Toyota; Dominic Chianese, actor, aka Uncle Jun on *The Sopranos*; Darlene Friedman, Soroptimist International; Ayumi Green, interpreter; Katherine Hahn, WebMD; Jeanne Mell, University City Science Center; Aki Nagunuma, translator; Todd Sommers, Best Western.

Special thanks go to Carole Alfano, communications director, New Hampshire State Senate. She has an amazing ability to make good things happen even under the tightest of deadlines.

My editor, Daniela Rapp, supported this new edition from the first day I mentioned it to her, and her editorial advice proved spot-on. Thank you. Thank you so much.

Steve Roman provided the copyediting, and his work was stellar. Quite simply, he provided the best copyediting any author could hope for. Many many thanks.

I want to express appreciation to my clients: In an era of increasingly large PR firms, your support of my independent speaker coaching and media training has allowed me to work at my professional best. Thank you for that privilege.

Finally, my deepest gratitude goes to my son, Seth Rubinstein, who grew up in my speechwriting business. Eight days after Seth was born, I resumed my speechwriting career—putting a baby swing in my home office so I could meet deadlines. Over the years, he's helped in my office in many ways: proofing, editing, making valuable suggestions. (Plus, I cannot begin to count

the number of times he has bailed me out of computer crises.)
Thank you, thank you. As written on the stone edifice of
your old Parrish Hall dorm at Swarthmore College: "On and
ever on."

PREFACE

How to Write & Give a Speech was first published in 1984. This is the third revised edition. I find it downright sobering that a modest two-page proposal was bought by St. Martin's Press thirty years ago and the book still keeps chugging along. Entire bookstore chains have closed their doors, independent bookstores struggle mightily to stay in business, e-book marketing has spent years predicting the demise of print—and yet, and yet, here we are. Readers still read. And this little title keeps going . . . now in both print and digital.

With each edition, I have (of course) made changes. But never have I made so many changes as this time.

What's different in the world since the previous edition? In a word: everything. Most especially, the way we communicate and the way we use technology. A client asked me last week, "What kind of speeches should I be giving in an age of tweets?" My short answer: "Very good speeches."

As I revised this edition, I kept my focus on the business aspects of both writing and giving speeches. That guided my updates. While some speakers may still think of a presentation as "filling fifteen minutes on the agenda," savvy speakers and speechwriters know better: Each presentation costs money, and we must make certain we're getting a good return on our speaking investment.

Let me ask a few questions.

- *If you give presentations:* Have you ever logged the hours you spend on preparation, rehearsal, and delivery? What's your time cost for giving a speech? More important, *what's your opportunity cost*? What are you *not* able to do because you spend

so much time researching, writing, stalling, rewriting, adding
PowerPoint, changing the PowerPoint, and then traveling to/
from all your speeches?

- *If you are an executive with a large corporation:* How much
  money does your corporation waste on mediocre speeches
  each year? Have you ever added up all the hours your employees spend *preparing* presentations . . . *giving* presentations . . . *attending* presentations? More important, have
  you ever questioned the return on your investment?

- *If you work in the public relations department of an organization:* Do you have a nagging suspicion your team could be
  writing better speeches—maybe even *much better* speeches?

- *If you are a small business owner or a consultant:* Do you worry
  about competing with larger businesses (who have larger advertising budgets)? Maybe you work on your own as an
  accountant or a fitness coach or an attorney. Maybe you run
  a unique store. How much business are you losing by not giving great presentations in the communities, associations, and
  industries you serve?

- *If you hire freelance speechwriters:* Do you think it's taking
  your freelancers too long to complete an assignment? Are you
  sick and tired of burning the midnight oil to rewrite their
  work?

- *If you are a public affairs officer with the government or the
  military:* Can you itemize all the meeting costs associated with
  a presentation? From an accountability standpoint, can you
  justify these costs? (Consider: Work hours? Conference room
  rentals? A-V fees? Coffee/tea service? Transportation? Lodg-
  ing?) On top of that, total the number of attendees. Add up the
  work hours they lose to attend a presentation. What a hefty
  dollar amount (or yen or pound or Euro amount) that must be!

I wrote this new edition with several goals in mind. I want this book to help you:

1. prepare *better* speeches in *less* time
2. give speeches that audiences remember
3. and (yes) give speeches that produce a return on your investment.

I want this book to help you look, feel, and sound terrific when you stand at a lectern.

Never forget: With technology that allows anyone to easily record you (and with the prospect that someone most likely will), a presentation on a given date in a given city takes on a timeless, global quality. You might think you're just talking to some people in San Antonio for about twenty minutes . . . but in a digital world, your recorded presentation can wind up anywhere and it can last forever.

So, here's the question: How do *you* wish to be seen in perpetuity? (It's enough to make you wish you had put more thought and practice into your presentation, eh?)

I'll wrap with a final observation:

In 2012, His Holiness the 14th Dalai Lama enthralled an audience at The College of William & Mary (my alma mater) in Williamsburg, Virginia. The arena held 8,200 people. When the public admission tickets for this speech went on sale, they were purchased in just sixteen minutes. Another 10,000 people watched online via Livestream. The audience—live and online—came from 109 nations.

The seventy-seven-year-old Buddhist spiritual leader, winner of the 1989 Nobel Peace Prize, gave a forty-five-minute presentation (wearing a green-and-gold William & Mary cap, no less) and then handled a thirty-five-minute question-and-answer session with aplomb. His theme? Love, compassion, and understanding.

I share this story for its lessons.

Few of us speakers will ever look out there and see 8,200 people leaning into our every word, hanging on our every pause. Few of us will ever give speeches that sell out in sixteen minutes. (Most presentations can only be described as "captive communications." Indeed, some speeches are so tedious, the audience would gladly *pay to leave*.) Few of us will be followed via Livestream. Few of us will be quoted throughout the world.

But we can all do better. Much, much, much better.

Every speaker can ramp up. Every speaker can raise their own performance bar—bit by bit.

Please remember this: When it comes to writing and giving a speech, *excellence costs no more than mediocrity*. I've been teaching this in my speechwriting seminars for more than twenty years: Choose excellence.

If you follow the advice in this book, you'll engage your audiences. You'll say something worth listening to. You'll give a speech that distinguishes your organization—and also distinguishes *you*.

Your speech will get noticed. And I promise: You will be remembered.

My good wishes for your success!
Joan Detz

How to Write &
Give a Speech

ONE

SO, YOU'VE BEEN ASKED TO GIVE A SPEECH. NOW WHAT?

A talk is a voyage. It must be charted. The speaker who starts nowhere, usually gets there.
—DALE CARNEGIE

It usually starts out simple: You get a phone call or an e-mail inviting you to speak at an event. Maybe your alma mater wants you to come back to campus and talk about your career. Maybe the local Chamber of Commerce just wants you to say a few words about your business at the chamber's next meeting. Maybe your favorite charitable organization wants you to stand up and share your expertise with the rest of the members.

But sometimes it's not so simple. Perhaps your boss wants you to give a presentation at a nationwide convention. Perhaps you're asked to participate in a podcast or a webinar. Perhaps your professional organization invites you to speak at an international conference.

What do you do?

Do you automatically say "yes" and then start scrambling to pull some remarks together?

Not if you're smart.

Remember: A speaking invitation is exactly that—it's an *invitation*. You have options. You get to decide if you:

- immediately accept the invitation exactly as they offered it (I don't recommend this)

- accept the invitation with some minor changes (for example, ask them if they can adjust the schedule a bit to accommodate your travel requirements)

- thank the conference chair for the invitation and say you'll need a few days to review your calendar before giving them an answer (this discreetly allows you to determine if the event is worth your while)

- let the organization know you'd love to speak with their members, but it's not possible this month (then suggest some months when your calendar would permit)

- graciously decline

The point is: It's an invitation, not a subpoena. And as the invited speaker, you have some choices.

The time to position yourself for speaking success is right now—when you first accept the invitation and set the terms of your talk. Why agree to speak for thirty minutes if you know you can cover the topic in fifteen? Why accept their 4 P.M. speaking slot (which will complicate your airport commute) when you can ask to speak at 2:30?

ONCE YOU'VE ACCEPTED, DETERMINE WHAT YOU WANT TO SAY

Begin by asking yourself, "What do I *really* want to say?" Then be ruthless in your answer. You have to focus your subject. You can't include everything in one speech.

Let me repeat that so it sinks in:

You can't include everything in one speech. In fact, if you try to include *everything,* your audience will probably come away with *nothing.* Decide what you really want to say, and don't throw in any other material.

For example, if you're speaking to a community group about your corporate ethics, don't think you have to give them a complete history of your company, too.

If you're speaking to an alumni group to raise funds for your university, don't throw in a section on the problems of America's high schools.

If you're speaking to a local school about the need for new foreign language studies, don't go off on a tangent about the principal's salary.

Get the picture? You're giving a speech, not a dissertation. You can't include every wise thought that's ever crossed your mind.

Remember Voltaire's observation: "The secret of being a bore is to tell everything."

WHAT TO DO IF YOU HAVE NOTHING TO SAY

Suppose that you can't think of anything to talk about.

Well, if you don't know what to say, ask yourself some basic questions about your department, your company, your industry, whatever. Think like a reporter. Dig for good material.

- *Who?* Who got us into this mess? Who can get us out? Who is really in charge? Who would benefit from this project? Who should get the credit for our success? Who should work on our team? Who will suffer if the merger fails?

- *What?* What does this situation mean? What actually happened? What went wrong? What is our current status? What do we want to happen? What will the future bring? What is our greatest strength? What is our biggest weakness?

- *Where?* Where do we go from here? Where can we get help? Where should we cut our budget? Where should we invest?

Where should we look for expertise? Where do we want to be in five years? Where can we expand operations? Where will the next problem come from?

- *When?* When did things start to go wrong? When did things start to improve? When did we first get involved? When will we be ready to handle a new project? When can the company expect to see progress? When will we make money? When will we be able to increase our staff?

- *Why?* Why did this happen? Why did we get involved? Why did we *not* get involved? Why did we get involved so late? Why do we let this mess continue? Why are we holding this meeting? Why should we stick with this course of action? Why should we continue to be patient? Why did they start that program?

- *How?* How can we get out of this situation? How did we ever get into it? How can we explain our position? How can we protect ourselves? How should we proceed? How should we spend the money? How will we develop our resources? How can we keep our good reputation? How can we improve our image? How does this program really work?

- *What if?* What if we could change the tax laws? What if we build another plant? What if the zoning regulations don't change? What if we expand into other subsidiaries? What if costs keep rising? What if we did better recruiting?

These questions should lead you to some interesting ideas. Need more inspiration? Visit a Web site from another field. Check out a blog with a different perspective. Read an academic journal from another discipline. Scan a magazine you don't normally read. Look at a foreign publication. Follow an RSS feed for a week or two. Join a new LinkedIn group to discover what others think. Do *something* to get a fresh perspective.

In short, welcome inspiration wherever you find it. The American painter Grant Wood once admitted, "All the really good ideas I ever had came to me while I was milking a cow."

Mystery writer Agatha Christie confessed she got her best ideas while doing the dishes.

Author Willa Cather sought inspiration by reading Biblical passages.

So, learn to keep your eyes and ears open. Take your good ideas wherever you can get them.

Think less about the past and more about the future. Thomas Jefferson said, "I like the dreams of the future better than the history of the past." Most audiences will feel the same way. Don't bore them with a five-year historical review of your industry. Instead, tell them how your industry will impact their own lives over the coming year.

One good way to focus your content: Ask yourself, "If I only had sixty seconds at that lectern, what would I absolutely have to say to get my message across?" There's nothing like a sixty-second limit to focus the mind!

Ask yourself, "What would interest this group?"

Media mogul Ted Turner once found himself in a situation where he was scheduled to give a speech in New York, but even en route to the city, he still had not decided on his message: "I just thought, what am I going to say?"

You can imagine the reaction from the dinner audience when Ted Turner announced he would give $1 billion to United Nations causes. Turner's speech didn't just make jaws drop in the audience. His speech transformed philanthropy.

Your speech doesn't have to give away $1 billion. But it should be interesting.

And it can't run long. I'll give Thomas Jefferson the last word: "Speeches that are measured by the hour will die with the hour."

TWO

ASSESSING YOUR AUDIENCE

Never treat your audience as customers, always as partners.

—JIMMY STEWART

Communication is a two-way street. Speakers shouldn't talk "at" audiences. Speakers need to talk "with" audiences. And the speakers who are wise enough to treat their audiences like partners in the communication process will fare much better.

This means: Speakers need to understand their audiences— and understand them well.

Harold Ross, in his 1925 prospectus for *The New Yorker*, summed up the magazine's content as "not edited for the old lady in Dubuque." That described his prospective reading audience quite nicely, but speakers facing a live audience will have to do a more detailed audience analysis.

Before you spend one minute researching your topic, before you write one word of your speech, first assess your audience. This chapter will give you a list of important questions to ask.

FAMILIARITY WITH THE SUBJECT

How much does the audience already know about the subject? Where did they get their information? How much more do they need or want to know?

For example: If you are a military speaker at a civilian forum, give your audience the background they need to understand your message. But don't overload the content. Don't hit them with too much data. You want this group to get your message—not be inundated by your messaging.

ATTITUDES

Why are these people coming to hear you speak? Are they *really* interested in the subject, or did someone (perhaps a boss or a professor) require them to attend? Will they be friendly, hostile, or apathetic?

A word of caution about "hostile" audiences: Don't be too quick to assume an audience will be hostile, and never give a speech with a chip on your shoulder.

Even if the audience doesn't agree with your viewpoint, they might appreciate your open-mindedness, your careful reasoning, and your balanced approach.

And besides . . . audiences can change their minds. In the words of William O. Douglas, who held the longest service in the history of the US Supreme Court: "The audience that hissed yesterday may applaud today, even for the same performance."

A word of advice about apathetic audiences: Some people won't be the least bit interested in your subject. Maybe they're in the audience just because they were obligated to attend, or because it was a chance to get out of the office for a while. Granted, *you* may be interested in your subject, but you'll find plenty of people who aren't.

Surprise them. Startle them. Wake them up. Use anecdotes, examples, and humor to keep their attention.

PRECONCEIVED NOTIONS

Will the audience have preconceived notions about you and your occupation? *Remember:* People are *never* completely objective. Emotion often overrules reason.

Try to imagine how the audience *feels* about you.

One effective way to make an impression on the audience is to shock them a bit—to confront and shatter their preconceptions. If you surprise their emotions, you may influence their reasoning.

For example, if you are a social worker, the audience may have a preconceived notion of you as a liberal, someone with no idea of what social services cost the taxpayer. Shatter this preconception. Talk about the need to cut administrative costs in social agencies. Talk about the need for stiffer penalties for those who abuse the system. Talk about the need for individual responsibility.

This approach will surprise—and probably impress—them. They will be more likely to *remember* your message.

SIZE

The size of an audience won't affect your subject matter, but it most certainly will affect your *approach* to the subject matter.

Small groups and large groups have different listening personalities and different psychological orientations. The wise speaker knows how to appeal to the needs of each group. People in small groups (say, up to fifteen or twenty people, maybe a board of directors, or a PTA committee) often know a lot about each other. They can frequently anticipate each other's reactions to new ideas.

People in small groups tend to pay closer attention to you because it's too risky for them to daydream. They may know you, and they may fear being caught off guard by an unexpected question from the podium such as, "I haven't been involved in this project, but I'm sure Paul Smith could tell us about that. Paul, would you be kind enough to stand up and give us the latest details?"

You can take advantage of this small-group attentiveness by emphasizing reason and by offering solid information.

People in large audiences *don't* normally know everyone else. It's easier for them to sit back and feel anonymous. It's also easier for them to daydream.

Speeches to a large audience can—indeed, often *should*—be more dramatic, more humorous, more emotional. Rhetorical devices that might seem contrived in a small group are now useful. The larger the crowd, the greater the need for "a good show."

People in large audiences tend to think, "Okay, recognize me, entertain me, inspire me. Make me feel good about myself when I leave here."

Cater to these needs.

Also, there's one other important reason to ask about the size—big or small—of an audience.

Obviously, if you assume several hundred people will attend, you may feel embarrassed and disappointed when only forty show up. On the other hand, consider this awful experience: A spokesperson for a health organization frequently spoke to small groups of nurses. One time she showed up at a convention and learned she had to speak to a couple of hundred nurses in a large auditorium. She didn't know how to use the microphone. Her PowerPoint wasn't bold enough for the new, large space. And she didn't have enough handouts. Is it any wonder she felt overwhelmed and nervous?

AGE

It's important to find out about the *age range* of an audience and to plan your speech accordingly.

What works for one age group could backfire mightily with another. For example, the military successfully uses repetition to tame antsy nineteen-year-olds, but that same training technique might fail with sixty-year-olds. (Several military aides once gave a repetitious slide show briefing to President Reagan—only to bring the lights up and find the president sound asleep, along with almost everyone else in the room.)

So, take a moment to think about the ages in your next audience.

Suppose, for example, you must represent your company at a special town meeting. The meeting starts at 7 P.M., and you expect whole families to attend—including parents with young children in tow.

Now, you may *plan* to talk to the homeowners in the audience about the need for new zoning regulations, but you must also be prepared for the pitter-patter of little feet running up and down the aisles and the cries of babies who want to be fed.

Realize that these distractions are inevitable, and that they will probably occur—alas—just when you get to the most critical part of your speech. If you are mentally prepared for these possibilities (and if you have some friendly one-liners ready), you will be less rattled when the disruptions occur.

Or, suppose you're talking with a group of college students. Pace your remarks to appeal to young people. Keep it lively. Keep it moving. And keep it brief. (If you can use great visuals, so much the better.)

MALE/FEMALE RATIO

Ask in advance about the likely male/female ratio, and use this information to help you prepare appropriate statistics and examples.

Be sure to cite appropriate sources as well. If you quote seven experts in your speech, but all seven are male, your oversight will be noticed. Instead, use balanced research that your audience will find credible.

ECONOMIC STATUS

Suppose you speak as a representative of the local electric utility. An affluent, community-minded group might appreciate hearing about your utility's contributions to cultural groups in the area. But people on fixed incomes won't be impressed to learn you give $30,000 each year to the local philharmonic. They would rather hear about specific ways to cut their electric bills or how your utility gives money to their local public libraries, where families can borrow free books and films each week.

EDUCATIONAL BACKGROUND

I once heard an engineer who spoke to all sorts of community groups about his corporation's projects. Unfortunately, he spoke the same way to graduate engineering students as he did to retirees who had no previous experience in the field. You can imagine how well his highly technical speeches went over with the retirees.

Of course, you don't need to change the *point* of your speech. Just talk at a level your audience can understand.

POLITICAL ORIENTATION

Even if you don't plan to address politics, it's important for you to understand any political preferences in this audience. Has the group taken an official stand on an important national issue? Did the group actively support a local candidate for office? Does the audience take a hard-and-fast view on certain issues?

When Pope John Paul II visited Cuba in 1998, his blunt message of freedom brought applause from the tens of thousands who had gathered for an open-air Mass in Santiago.

In 2011, when U.S. Secretary of State Hillary Rodham Clinton delivered a historic speech on LGBT rights, she acknowledged the political sensitivities of the issue, but she declared unequivocally that LGBT rights are the same as racial equality and rights for women:

"All people deserve to be treated with dignity and have their human rights respected, no matter who they are or whom they love."

CULTURAL LIFE

On a Sunday afternoon, would your audience be more likely to visit a museum, shop online, or take their kids to a park? Would your audience read *The Economist, Good Housekeeping,* or *Wired* magazine?

All of this information will help you understand your audience. When you understand your audience, you'll give a better speech. Plus (and this is a great bonus) you'll have a much easier time with the question-and-answer session.

But, how can you *get* this information about your audience—and get it quickly? Here are eleven tips:

1. *Start by visiting the organization's Web site.* Get background information, so you'll have a good working knowledge of the group prior to any discussions.

2. *Talk with the person who invited you to speak.* If that person is too busy to help, ask for the name and number of someone who can spend more time with you. *Don't* settle for a fact sheet from a Web site. A fact sheet won't give you insight into the personality of the audience.

3. *Ask to see the evaluation forms from previous events.* What did previous audiences like best? Least?

4. *Talk with previous speakers, if possible.* See what their experiences were like. What worked? What didn't? What would the speakers do differently if they had a second chance?

5. *Talk with someone who will be in the audience.* What are these meetings usually like? Does anything particularly frustrate the attendees? Perhaps limited parking causes them to arrive late, or the small size of the room is uncomfortable. You won't know until you ask.

   I once attended a marvelous presentation at a historical society, but the large crowd kept me from getting a seat inside the room—I listened from the vestibule. In addition, the group's overflow parking spilled into an adjacent lot, which happened to belong to a funeral home. I'm not making this up: When the presentation was about 90 percent complete (and it was so good, we were hanging on every word, every visual), the program was interrupted with an announcement that we'd have to move our cars from the funeral establishment's parking lot as quickly as possible because a funeral service was about to begin. The audience ran out—literally. Attendees had no chance to linger with a Q&A, and the speaker never got to give the ending he had planned.

See what I mean? The smallest, most mundane detail can wreak havoc with an otherwise wonderful presentation. Learn about these details before they do you in.

6. *Ask their public relations people.* Can they share useful information about the organization?

7. *Contact the officers of the organization.* But take their information with the proverbial grain of salt. Officers give "official" information, and rarely provide the candid observations you need.

8. *If it's an out-of-town speech, visit the chamber of commerce Web site to get some local perspectives on the area.*

9. *Participate in social media.* Ask questions. Follow discussions. But don't tip your hand too much. You want to deliver your message fresh to a live audience—and not leak it online.

10. *Use common sense.* Think. Just sit and think about the audience. Try to look at your topic from their perspective.

11. *Above all, use a little imagination.* Curiosity will bring its own rewards. As Albert Einstein advised, "The important thing is not to stop questioning. Curiosity has its own reason for existing."

AN ADDITIONAL WORD TO THE WISE

It's not smart to give the same speech to different audiences. Why?

- You will eventually get tired of presenting the same material, and your boredom will show.

- No two audiences are alike. Your listeners will have different attitudes, special interests, and pet peeves. A direct proportion exists here: The more you try to lump all of your audiences together, the more they will disregard—perhaps even dislike—you.

- You never know if someone in the audience might have heard you give the identical speech somewhere else.

Improbable? Think about this embarrassing situation. One Monday morning at New York's Waldorf Astoria hotel, a minister pronounced the benediction before a breakfast meeting of the American Newspaper Publishers Association.

Later in the day, he returned to the Waldorf Astoria to give the blessing at an Associated Press luncheon. It was—you guessed it—the same prayer, and listeners who attended both meetings could pick up the repeated phrases.

Even worse, *The New York Times* was quick to pick up the story, and ran it under the headline "Invoking the Familiar."

Funny? Sure—as long as it happens to some other speaker and not to you.

PRE-PRESENTATION AUDIENCE ANALYSIS

Early in your preparation process, learn as much as you can about your audience. Tracking down this information early on will save you both time and frustration.

1. How many people will attend this program?
2. Age range?
3. Male/female ratio?
4. Educational backgrounds?
5. Cultural backgrounds?
6. How much do they already know about me/my organization?
7. a) Where did they get this information (or misinformation)?

    b) When did they get this information (or misinformation)?
8. How can I correct any misconceptions they might have?
9. a) What details about my general work would capture their interest?

    b) What details about my specific topic would interest them?
10. What information sources would have the most credibility for this group?

THREE

WHERE AND WHEN WILL YOU SPEAK?

The most dangerous phrase in the language is,
"We've always done it this way."
—REAR ADMIRAL GRACE HOPPER

I've learned to pay close attention to the location and timing of any speech ever since my early days as a professional speechwriter. It was my job to plan some remarks that would be delivered at a landfill. (You read that correctly: a landfill.) I thought I had anticipated everything, but I neglected to consider one factor: the gulls. Honking gulls. Swooping gulls. By the dozens.

Yes, I had certainly planned to keep the remarks brief, but as I soon learned: No speech can be brief enough when you're speaking at a landfill with dive-bombing gulls.

Learn from my mistake.

As soon as you have determined what your audience will be like, your next step is to consider where and when you will give your speech. Pay full attention to this part of the process.

Don't start researching the topic. Don't worry about organizing the material. Don't even think about writing the speech. At this early stage, you need to focus on *exactly where* and *exactly when* you will speak.

WHERE

Let's start with the basics. Where, *exactly,* will you give the speech?

- In the training center of a large corporation?
- In a university auditorium?
- In a tiny town hall meeting room?
- In a high school classroom?
- In a hotel conference room?
- In a theater?
- In a gymnasium?
- In a restaurant?
- On an outdoor platform?

Does it make any difference? Yes.

PLAN A SPEECH THAT'S APPROPRIATE TO THE SETTING

For example:

- If you're speaking on an outdoor platform (as is common at graduations), be sensitive to the weather. Know how to "wrap up" your speech in a hurry if a June thunderstorm cuts you short.
- If you must speak in a large banquet hall, have some one-liners ready for the inevitable moments when waiters interrupt your speech to serve coffee and drown out your words with the clatter of dishes.

- If you'll be in a hotel conference room, bring along some signs reading, "Quiet please—Meeting in progress." Post these signs on the doors to alert people passing through the corridor. (You'll be glad you took this precaution.)

- If you've never seen the location in person, check it online. Ask the program host about the room's details. Where will you stand? Where will the audience sit? Are the chairs movable? Will food be served, and if so, where will that buffet be set up?

"Seeing" all this ahead of time will help you feel more comfortable when you actually speak there.

Are you traveling to an out-of-town location? Due diligence. Consider not just the location of your speech, but find out what's nearby.

Will you be giving a speech down the road from a historical monument, or a famous university, or an Air Force base, or a literary statue, or a noted research park? If so, perhaps you can incorporate that into the opening of your speech.

TIE THE LOCATION INTO THE THEME OF YOUR SPEECH

President Barack Obama chose to give the first major foreign policy speech of his presidency in Prague. On that spring day in 2009, President Obama opened by referring to the statue behind him:

Behind me is a statue of a hero of the Czech people—Tomas Masaryk. In 1918, after America had pledged its support for Czech independence, Masaryk spoke to a crowd in Chicago that was estimated to be over 100,000. I don't think I can match his record [laughter] but I am honored to follow his footsteps from Chicago to Prague.

For over a thousand years, Prague has set itself apart from any other city in any other place. You've known war and peace. You've seen empires rise and fall. You've led revolutions in the arts and science, in politics and in poetry. Through it all, the people of Prague have insisted on pursuing their own path, and defining their own destiny. . . .

Olli-Pekka Kallasvuo, as chairman of Nokia, addressed a standing-room only audience at the 2010 Consumer Electronics Show, which is always held in Las Vegas. Notice how he used the location of his speech to draw attention to his message:

Vegas, of course, is dedicated to the pursuit of fun and games. It was designed to be an unreal world—a city of escape. What I want to do this morning is take you to a very different, very real world.

It's the world where most of Earth's inhabitants live. And most of it is about as far from the glitz of the Strip as you can imagine. It's a world in which millions of people face a daily struggle just to survive.

But it's also a world of increasing opportunity and upward mobility, where wealth is being created at an incredible rate, where innovation is thriving, where business opportunities abound, and where the future is brighter than it has ever been.

Mobile communications have played a big role in bringing hope and higher living standards to billions of people. This trend promises to accelerate as the capabilities of smartphones spread across the globe . . . .

WHEN

You may delay, but time will not.

—BEN FRANKLIN

Again, the basics. When, *exactly,* will you give the speech?

- At a breakfast meeting?
- At a mid-morning seminar?
- Just before lunch?
- During lunch, with servers jostling plates while you speak?
- After lunch, before people return to work?
- As part of a mid-afternoon panel?
- At 4 P.M., as the final speaker in the day's seminar?
- At 9 P.M., as the after-dinner speaker?
- At 11 P.M., as the last in a string of after-dinner speakers?

PLAN A SPEECH THAT SUITS THE TIME OF DAY

Use your imagination. Always look at the event from the audience's perspective. What will be on *their* minds?

For example:

- You must be especially brief and succinct at a breakfast meeting. Why? Because your breakfast meeting forced the audience to get up an hour or two early, and it also forced them to change their morning commute. Plus, they still face a whole day's work ahead of them. If your speech isn't interesting, they will be particularly disappointed. If your speech is not clear and concise—and if they can't get to their offices on time—they will flat-out resent you.

- If you speak on a mid-afternoon panel, find out whether you'll speak first or last. Panel presentations run notoriously behind schedule, and the last speaker often feels "squeezed" for time. Be realistic, and be prepared to give a shortened presentation, if necessary.

Anthropologist Edward Hall devoted his career to understanding people's use of "time." Consider this observation by Hall in his 1959 work, *The Silent Language*:

> . . . plant managers in the United States are fully aware of the significance of a communication made during the middle of the morning or afternoon that takes everyone away from his work. Whenever they want to make an important announcement, they will ask: "When shall we let them know?"

If you speak after a banquet (perhaps to celebrate a retirement), know that the audience has been eating and drinking for several hours. They will be in a good mood. They will want to *stay* in a good mood. Don't ruin their evening with an overly long, overly serious speech.

Adlai Stevenson got it right when he said, "The best after-dinner speech I ever heard was, 'Waiter, I'll take the check.'"

SHOULD YOU REQUEST A PARTICULAR TIME SLOT?

Yes, if it will improve the effect of your speech. Suppose, for example, you learn that you're scheduled to speak after a series of award presentations. You suspect, and rightly so, that the audience will be restless after hearing all those thank-you speeches. What should you do?

- Be assertive. Let the program host know that you're willing to listen to the award presentations, but that you're not willing to follow them.

- If you are showing PowerPoint and will require a darkened room, ask to speak mid-morning. Avoid darkened rooms immediately after lunch or dinner. They are conducive to sleep—and the last thing you want is to have your speech interrupted by snores.

A NOTE ABOUT MEDIA ATTENTION

By choosing the timing and the location of your message with some creativity, you can capture more attention.

For example, when Mars, Inc., announced a much ballyhooed color addition to its beloved M&M chocolate candies in 1995, they unveiled the new blue M&M at the Empire State Building—which was duly lighted in blue for the occasion.

When Kraft celebrated the hundredth birthday of its beloved Oreo cookie in 2012, the Shanghai waterfront was turned into a vast Oreo advertisement (replete with fireworks) . . . flash mobs in seven U.S. cities burst into stirring renditions of "Happy Birthday" . . . Venezuela showed hundredth birthday gusto with piñata-breaking. Social media was alive with crowd-sourced photos of happy Oreo-eaters.

When Hasbro decided to replace a token on its iconic Monopoly board in 2013, the company held a vote on Facebook, marking the first time that fans had a say on the game's eight tokens. Fans from more than 120 countries voted. Hasbro announced the news from its corporate headquarters in Rhode Island, letting the world know that a cat would replace the iron.

CONNECT THE DATE OF THE SPEECH
TO YOUR THEME

On October 31, 2011, when Shell CEO Peter Voser addressed the Singapore Energy Summit, Earth became home to the 7 billionth person. Voser used this landmark "day in history" moment to open his energy message:

> Today, our world reached a significant milestone: Somewhere—most likely here in Asia—a mother gave birth to Earth's 7 billionth inhabitant.
>
> Of course, we'll never know for sure who the 7 billionth person is. We'll never know exactly where he or she was born. But based on computer projections from the United Nations, today is that child's birthday.

FOUR

HOW TO RESEARCH A SPEECH

If we knew what we were doing, it wouldn't be called research, would it?

–ALBERT EINSTEIN

Now that you've determined the nature of your audience and considered where and when you will speak, the next step is to gather information for your speech. But don't rush to accumulate data. Instead, just sit down and *think*.

USE YOUR HEAD

Your best information source is always *your own head*. Ask yourself, "What do I *already* know about this subject?" Then jot down your thoughts.

Don't worry about organization at this point, just make some rough notes. Write down important facts, opinions, ideas—whatever information you already know. Let your notes sit for a day or two, if possible. Then review them.

Now, begin to identify *specific* information in the form of statistics, quotations, examples, definitions, case histories, references to pop culture, comparisons, and contrasts—in short, come up with details to support your overall message.

Equally important: If your details don't have enough variety, fix that problem. You can't shove thirty-eight statistics into a speech and think you're done. You need a variety of research: a few statistics, a clever definition, some good examples, a quick reference to the day's news, a personal anecdote, a professional opinion. Get the idea? You want a broad selection of research to keep the audience's attention.

Need some help? Turn to the Research Checklist at the end of this chapter.

WHAT TO LEAVE OUT

As the speaker, you're in control: *You* get to choose the precise topic. You also get to decide what information stays and what information goes. What *not* to say is just as important as what *to* say.

Leave out:

- irrelevant details

- boring details

- any information you can't verify

- anything you wouldn't want to see quoted in print the next day

- anything you wouldn't want to be reminded of next year

APPROACH THE TOPIC FROM THE AUDIENCE'S PERSPECTIVE

Your audience can understand your subject only by relating it to their own ideas and problems and experiences. So, approach the subject from *their* perspective, not *your* perspective.

For example, don't just complain about your organization's problems. Even if you have some legitimate complaints, your audience will probably not care very much. They have enough problems of their own.

Instead, relate *your* concerns to *their* concerns. Find the emotional "hook" that will help an audience understand your message.

Talk about audience *benefits*. Show how the audience would benefit if your organization could improve its situation.

For example: Suppose you're doing fund-raising presentations for your local library. If the library could raise extra funds, how would the audience benefit? Would they enjoy longer library hours . . . Sunday access . . . a children's reading hour . . . a business and career center?

Approach the topic from the audience's perspective, and you'll be more effective. Audiences tend to trust—and like—speakers who show a real understanding of them.

HOW TO USE STATISTICS FOR IMPACT

Some people think statistics are boring. These people have not heard the right statistics.

Statistics can be downright interesting, if you:

1. *Make the statistics seem real to your audience.* Try, "While we're sitting here for an hour and debating the value of sex education in the schools, 'x number' of teenagers will have babies while they are still children themselves."

   Or, "While you're watching your favorite TV show tonight, forty-five people will call our cocaine hot line to ask for help. Could one of those callers be *your* child?"

2. *Put statistics in simple terms.* Don't just say that your senator will mail "x" million items to her constituents this year. Instead, explain that this amounts to about three deliveries to every mailbox in her district. Everyone who has a mailbox can relate to that statistic.

3. *Round off the numbers.* Say "almost one million customers," not "997,755 customers." Make it easy for the audience to *hear and remember* your statistics.

4. *Use numbers sparingly.* Audiences cannot absorb more than a few numbers at a time. If you use too many statistics, you will lose your listeners.

When Soroptimist International speaks about its work to improve the lives of women and girls around the world, they use a compelling narrative but relatively few statistics. The few numbers they do use are carefully chosen for power and impact. Consider these statistics from a 2013 Soroptimist speech:

- Of all the people trafficked across international borders, 79 percent are female.

- One in three women have been beaten, coerced into sex, or otherwise abused in their lifetime.

- Two-thirds of the 880 million illiterate adults are women.

5. *Put statistics in perspective.* Here's how David Kong, CEO of Best Western, used statistics to illustrate the company's strong social media presence:

We were an early adopter of social media. Our Facebook presence has about half a million Likes—the most in the industry. Our YouTube videos have two and a half times the industry average number of views.

We have 44 percent overall share of followers on Twitter, far more than any other brand. It's no wonder Cornell Hotel School's social media report said, "Best Western has the strongest social media presence overall."

6. *Be graphic.* Try to paint a picture with numbers. Say, "It's as long as four football fields." Or, "The stack of papers would be as tall as the bank building across the street." Or, "It would fill a hole big enough to hold 100 train cars."

My point is: Let your audience *see* your numbers by using real-life examples.

7. *Put any time references* before *the statistics.* Consider this

example from a speech given by Shigeki Terashi, as Toyota's North American manufacturing president:

In early 2012, we began a series of production shifts from Japan to North America. We announced capacity expansions in Indiana, West Virginia, Missouri, Kentucky, Alabama, and two in Canada. These expansions represent $1.5 billion in new investment and more than 3,500 new jobs.

A quick exercise: Read that first sentence aloud. Did you notice how helpful it was to hear "in early 2012" at the very beginning? Follow this speechwriting technique: Let listeners hear the time frame *before* they hear the statistics.

8. *Do not apologize for using statistics.* Inexperienced speakers often say, "I hate to bore you with statistics, but . . ." After this apology, they proceed to bore their audiences with poorly chosen and poorly used statistics.

    Avoid this pitfall. If you follow the guidelines in this chapter, your statistics will *not* be boring. They will, in fact, add a lot of interest to your speech.

HOW TO USE QUOTATIONS

Next to the originator of a good sentence is the first quoter of it.

—RALPH WALDO EMERSON

Audiences love quotations, if you:

1. *Use a quote that has rhetorical clout.* In his acceptance speech as presidential candidate, Jimmy Carter cited Winston Churchill's remark: "We have not journeyed all this way across the centuries, across the oceans, across the

mountains, across the prairies, because we are made of sugar candy."

2. *Blend the quotation into the text.* Don't say, "quote . . . unquote." Instead, pause a moment and let your voice emphasize the quotation.

   The Office of Lt. Governor Anthony Brown of Maryland prepared a keynote address for Black History Month in 2007 and used this short, powerful quote: "Every single one of us . . . has a responsibility to fulfill and promote the American Dream. In the words of Frederick Douglass, 'Power concedes nothing without a demand. It never did and it never will.'"

3. *Avoid lengthy or complicated quotations.* Keep quotations short. Cut or paraphrase any "slow parts."

4. *Choose a source who has relevance for the topic and the audience.* When Mario Draghi, president of the European Central Bank, spoke at the Frankfurt [Germany] Chamber of Commerce and Industry in 2013, he quoted Walter Hallstein, who had served as the first president of the European Commission: ". . . anyone who does not believe in miracles in European matters is not a realist."

5. *Appear comfortable with the quotation.* Never quote anybody unless you're sure you can pronounce the name right. I once heard a speaker quote "the well-known German writer, Goethe." Unfortunately, he pronounced the name as "Goath"—and the quotation just fell flat (as did the speaker's credibility).

6. *Tap into the emotional impact of a quotation.* When King George VI gave his Christmas message in 1939, he ended by citing a few lines from a poem that he had just seen.

   "And I said to the man who stood at the gate of the year: 'Give me a light that I may tread safely into the unknown.'

And he replied: "'Go out into the darkness and put your hand into the Hand of God. That shall be to you better than light and safer than a known way.'"

Then King George VI ended with this one-line blessing: "May that Almighty hand guide and uphold us all."

A note to my fellow history buffs: Written by Minnie Louise Haskins, an instructor at the London School of Economics, "The Gate of the Year" became hugely popular throughout Britain after the king quoted it in his Christmas speech. It was particularly beloved by his wife, Queen Elizabeth. As I watched the Queen Mother's state funeral in 2002, I heard those poetic lines read aloud—at her request.

7. *Use quotations judiciously.* A speech should reflect *your* thoughts and expertise, so don't quote dozens of other people. In a fifteen-minute speech, you can comfortably use one or two quotations. *Remember:* The impact of your quotations will decline sharply as their number grows.

HOW TO USE DEFINITIONS

Definitions are underused. Too many speakers overuse statistics and ignore the power of definitions. That's too bad, because great definitions add so much to a speech.

Consider these guidelines:

1. *Define your terms in everyday words.* Avoid "dictionary" definitions. "According to Webster . . ." is a phrase that sounds feeble and amateurish.

2. *Consult the Appendix of this book for sources of lively definitions.*

   • Sir John Quinton (British banker): "Politicians are people who, when they see light at the end of the tunnel, go out and buy some more tunnel."

- James J. Walker (former mayor of New York City): "A reformer is a guy who rides through a sewer in a glass-bottomed boat."
- Groucho Marx: "Politics is the art of looking for trouble, finding it everywhere, diagnosing it incorrectly, and applying the wrong remedies."
- Jimmy Carter: "The present tax structure is . . . just a welfare program for the rich."

3. *Define your organization in your own way and with your own terms.*

I was impressed by a speech delivered by Stephen S. Tang, Ph.D., the CEO of University City Science Center. Speaking in Delaware in 2012, Dr. Tang considered the importance of science centers to the vitality of a region and defined Philadelphia's University City Science Center with these words:

> "As the oldest and largest urban research park in the nation, the Science Center has supported innovation and entrepreneurship in the region since 1963. Or to put it more simply, we've been inventing the future for fifty years."

HOW TO USE PROVERBS

In 2013, with Vice President Joe Biden and families from Newtown, Connecticut, by his side, New York City mayor Michael Bloomberg spoke about the need for common-sense federal gun laws, using a proverb to illustrate the lesson:

> There is a Jewish proverb which tells us that "remembrance is the secret of redemption." The lesson is: If we ignore the horrors of the past, we are doomed to repeat them. But if we remember them—and if we learn from them—we can redeem ourselves from their grip.

That's why all of us are here today: Because we believe that we have a responsibility to help free our country from the gun violence that takes lives and breaks hearts every single day all year round. . . .

HOW TO USE COMPARISONS AND CONTRASTS

Use everyday comparisons to which people can easily relate. When Leo Durocher was manager of the Brooklyn Dodgers, he was booed for pulling a pitcher out late in a close game. Afterward, a reporter asked him how he felt about the crowd's reaction. Durocher's comparison? "Baseball is like church. Many attend. Few understand."

In his farewell address as mayor of New York City, Rudolph Giuliani compared the World Trade Center to a great battlefield. Speaking adjacent to the rubble at Ground Zero, Giuliani said, "This is going to be a place that is remembered one hundred and one thousand years from now, like the great battlefields of Europe and of the United States . . . Normandy or Valley Forge or Bunker Hill or Gettysburg."

In 2012, the American Chamber of Commerce in Slovakia held a seminar on "Data Protection and Cyber Security." I was travelling in Bratislava shortly after the event and happened to notice the publicity. U.S. ambassador H.E. (His Excellency) Theodore Sedgwick gave the keynote address, emphasizing the need for the United States and the European Union to share compatible privacy rules. Why? So data can flow across borders just as freely as people and goods. Ambassador Sedgwick compared Slovakia's economy with other countries: "Slovakia has the fastest growing economy in Europe right now."

HOW TO USE EXAMPLES

Specific examples will help your message "stick" in the audience's mind.

In an address to the nation on stem cell research, President George W. Bush used the power of personal examples: "I have friends whose children suffer from juvenile diabetes. Nancy Reagan has written me about President Reagan's struggle with Alzheimer's. My own family has confronted the tragedy of child-hood leukemia."

HOW TO USE ANECDOTES

Audiences love good anecdotes. Even more important, they love the speakers who tell them.

The Appendix of this book lists many books and Web sites where you can find great anecdotes. But you don't need to spend hours on the Internet or in a library. Some of the best research details will spring from your own experience.

"The Great Communicator," Ronald Reagan, certainly knew the power of a good anecdote. Here's a brief personal story he shared in 1984 with the National Association of Evangelicals:

> During World War II, I remember a rally to promote war bonds that was held at Madison Square Garden in New York. The rally featured great figures. And then [the audience] remained for a $54-a-month buck private who spoke nine words that no one there that day will ever forget. His name was Joe Louis—yes, the Joe Louis who had come from the cotton fields to become the world heavyweight prize-fighting champion. Now, this $54-a-month private walked out to center stage after all those other celebrities had been there, and he said, "I know we'll win, because we're on God's side." There was a moment of silence, and then that crowd nearly took the roof off.

Norman Mineta, former U.S. secretary of transportation, drew on his own painful experiences as an American of Japanese ancestry when he spoke at the University of Rochester just weeks after the 9/11 attack on America. Mineta described the terrible treatment of Japanese-Americans during World War II, and urged people not to mistreat Arab- and Muslim-Americans in the wake of the terrorist attacks. Mineta's personal story strengthened his political message.

SOME FINAL THOUGHTS
ABOUT RESEARCH

Sophisticated listeners will question the source of your information. Make sure each source is *reputable* and *appropriate* for your particular audience. Again, each audience is different. Use different sources to meet their needs.

I want to reiterate: Be sure to use a *mixture* of material in your speech—maybe one or two quotations, an example, a couple of bold statistics, a clever definition, a comparison, and perhaps a reference to the day's news. This variety will make your speech more interesting, more credible, and more quote worthy.

Be aware: Some people just don't assimilate certain types of information. "Numbers people" may consider personal anecdotes to be somewhat frivolous. "People people" may mistrust statistics, preferring to receive their information in anecdotal form.

Use a combination of techniques so you can get your message across to everyone in the audience.

As Bette Midler describes the way she puts together an effective show, "I always try to balance the light with the heavy—a few tears for the human spirit in with the sequins and the fringes."

That same balance can work to the advantage of anyone trying to gather research for a speech. The *variety* can prove powerful— and create a more memorable speech.

RESEARCH: USE VARIETY

Use this checklist to identify the types of research you're using in your speech. Quantify your research. Too many speakers find they use lots of statistics or lots of quotations, but nothing else. If you find yourself relying on only two or three kinds of research, then make a concerted effort to add variety.

- ☐ anecdotes
- ☐ case histories
- ☐ charts
- ☐ comparisons & contrasts
- ☐ date in history
- ☐ definitions
- ☐ demonstrations
- ☐ endorsements
- ☐ examples
- ☐ experts
- ☐ graphs

- ☐ interviews (audio clips, video clips)
- ☐ letters (from customers, the community, elected officials, vendors, etc)
- ☐ news stories
- ☐ polls
- ☐ pop culture references
- ☐ props
- ☐ quotations
- ☐ statistics

FIVE

WRITING THE SPEECH

*A writer's working hours are his waking hours.
He is working as long as he is conscious and
frequently when he isn't.*

—EDNA FERBER

All right. Enough thinking, enough planning, enough research-ing. Now's the time to sit down and write.

What do you have to do to write a good speech? Two things:

1. Make it simple.
2. Make it short.

What do you have to do to write a *great* speech?

1. Make it simpler.
2. Make it shorter.

In this chapter, I'll tell you how to make your speech simple and easy to understand. In the next chapter, I'll show you specific techniques to make it memorable.

These two chapters are the guts of the book. Read them care-fully. Reread them with a pencil in your hand. Mark them up. Because they tell you everything this professional speechwriter knows about writing speeches.

THE NEVER-FAIL FORMULA

Here's the formula for a successful speech. It works every time.

- Tell them what you're going to tell them.
- Tell them.
- Tell them what you've told them.

TELL THEM WHAT YOU'RE GOING TO TELL THEM: THE OPENING

I won't mince words. The opening is the toughest part. If you don't hook your listeners within the first thirty seconds, your cause is probably lost.

Start with a "grabber"—an anecdote, a startling statistic, a quotation, a personal observation, or a reference to the location. Use whatever it takes to get the audience's attention.

Give them a good taste of what's to come. It can be risky to begin a speech with a joke. If it falls flat, you're off to a terrible start, so don't use a joke unless you are *absolutely* sure you can deliver it well. Even then, use a joke only if it's short and if it relates to the topic of the speech.

Never, *never,* open by saying something like, "I heard a really funny story today. It doesn't have anything to do with my speech, but at least it'll give you a good laugh."

Instead, try one of these opening techniques:

TAKE A YOU-ORIENTED APPROACH

Use the word "you" as much as possible. It builds rapport between the speaker and the audience. It also helps build a bond among audience members, so everyone feels a part of the same event and shares an interest in the same issues.

In 2012, Dr. Hansa Bhargava, a WebMD pediatrician, spoke at First Lady Michelle Obama's town hall meeting in Homestead, Florida. Hosted by WebMD, the town hall aimed to help families live healthier lives. Dr. Bhargava focused on childhood obesity. Notice how often she used the word "you" to engage her audience:

> . . . it's not only what kinds of foods you eat, but also when you eat them and how you eat them. It's important to sit down and eat them, not in front of a television, so that you know what you're eating and you enjoy your food. And remember: always have as many family meals as possible, because that will make you healthy and happy.

USE SHORT WORDS

Here is how New Hampshire Senator John "Jack" Barnes Jr. opened a commencement address:

> I want every graduate here to know: you always have options.
>   You can stay or you can go. You can focus on the negative or stress the positive. You can hold a grudge or let it fade away. You can choose kind words over criticism. You can stay on a rough road or start on a new path. You can speak up, or be silent.

A quick exercise: Notice his effective use of short words. Count the number of letters per word in this excerpt. Many words have only three or four letters.

USE LOCAL DETAILS

When Bill Dahlberg, as CEO of the Southern Company, spoke to the DeKalb (Georgia) Chamber of Commerce, he opened with this local connection:

Fifty years ago, my father moved our family to a little unincorporated community, just southwest of Stone Mountain, called Mountainview. The biggest thing there was Hiram Crow's store. If you went down the road another quarter of a mile, you'd come to Louis Crow's store. If you went a little bit further down the road, you'd come to Jay Crow's Dairy and Store. It may have been the first mom-and-pop chain in all of DeKalb County. My first three years in school were spent in a two-room schoolhouse. I believe we had a coal stove for heat. I do know the bathrooms were outside. DeKalb County now, of course, has huge schools—huge, overcrowded schools— schools with trailers in back. Air-conditioned trailers, I might add.

MAKE A REFERENCE TO THE DATE

Giving a speech on June 14? Find out what happened on that date in history and see if it connects to the theme of your speech. The "date in history" technique is catchy, clever, and irresistibly quotable to the press. Even better, it's quick and easy to prepare.

The Appendix at the back of this book gives detailed listings about Web sites and reference books that tell "what happened on this date in history." You'll want to bookmark these resources.

CITE YOUR PROFESSIONAL CREDENTIALS–OR YOUR PERSONAL CREDENTIALS–OR, EVEN BETTER, BOTH

E. James Morton, now former CEO of John Hancock Mutual Life Insurance Company, once spoke to the National Conference on Work and Family Issues and created a strong rapport with this opening:

Well, my instructions were to be as provocative and visionary as I can. . . . I am, by training, an actuary. A common definition is that an actuary is someone who didn't have enough personality to be an accountant. Provocativeness and vision are not normally in our bag of tricks. But, we do know a little bit about demographics and how to project trends, so let me do the best I can per instructions.

I might also add, on a personal basis, that my own situation does give me a fairly broad range of experience in family matters. I have a ninety-year-old mother; three daughters whose ages are forty-one, twenty-six, and eight; a nine-month-old grandson; and a baby-boomer wife whose mother is a World War II Icelandic war bride, and who lives in another city to which I commute on weekends. So I believe that I can relate closely to practically any demographic or family situation that anyone can bring up.

OPENINGS FOR SPECIAL CIRCUMSTANCES

If you are a substitute speaker:

So, you're a last-minute invitee? Get it out in the open, and move on. Don't belabor the fact.

Yes, they may have been expecting someone else, but if you're interesting, they'll be very glad to *hear you*. Really.

If you are speaking out of town:

Avoid this all-too-common opening: "It's great being here in Cincinnati/Philadelphia/Walla Walla."

The first thing your audience wants to know is "Why?" "Why on earth," they're saying to themselves, "are you so thrilled to be here in Cincinnati/Philadelphia/Walla Walla?" Were you born here? Did you go to college here? Did you start your first job here? If so, then *tell* the audience. They'll appreciate the personal connection.

If you're the last to speak:

Keep it brief, and make it lively. *Remember:* The poor audience has been sitting there listening to speech after speech—each possibly more tedious than the one before! So, give them a break, and let them end on an upbeat.

One time, George Bernard Shaw had to follow a series of speakers, and he took this approach: After he was introduced and the applause subsided, he simply said, "Ladies and gentlemen: The subject may not be exhausted, but we are." With that summation, he sat down.

There might be a lesson in that. Of course, in the business of professional speaking (where luminaries such as Oprah Winfrey can command $100,000 per speech, and Bill Clinton can command $200,000), the audience expects to hear the speech they paid for.

But for the rest of us? George Bernard Shaw's advice could come in useful.

SOME CAUTIONS ABOUT BEGINNING A SPEECH

It's not necessary—or even desirable—to begin with, "Good evening, ladies and gentlemen." Greetings like this are really just fillers. Skip them. Jump right in with the first line of your speech.

The same goes with most introductory thank-yous. They can sound pretty feeble, and feeble is not the way to begin a speech. Whatever you do, avoid trite openings. Almost every run-of-the-mill (read: boring) speech begins with something like, "It's such a wonderful pleasure to be here today." Who is this speaker trying to kid? Since when is speechmaking such a pleasure?

Everyone knows that giving a speech is hard work. Most people would rather do *anything* than stand up and give a speech.

Don't flash a phony smile and open with a glib line. Audiences are quick to spot insincerity—and they're slow to forgive you for it.

If you're really enthusiastic about giving your speech, it will show in your content and delivery. You won't have to fake it with flowery openings.

TELL THEM: THE BODY

Organizing is what you do before you do something,
so that when you do it, it is not all mixed up.
—CHRISTOPHER ROBIN IN
A. A. MILNE'S *WINNIE-THE-POOH*

Inexperienced speechwriters want to say everything, and that's where they make their first mistake. Focus your material, and limit the number of points you make.

If you concentrate on one central idea, your audience will stand a better chance of getting your message.

If you are thinking, "But my topic is so important, I've *got* to get everything across" . . . well, that's a sharp clue you're headed for trouble.

If you try to say *everything* in a speech, your audience will come away with *nothing*. It's as simple as that.

No matter what your speech is about, you must limit, focus, and organize your material. There are lots of ways to do this. Use whatever method works best for you.

CHRONOLOGICAL ORDER

Try dividing your material into time units—from past to present to future—or whatever pattern seems to fit. This method can be effective because it *connects* everything.

Show how historical changes affect the quality of people's lives. If possible, show how these changes affect the quality of your *audience's* lives.

CAUSE AND EFFECT

Did your environmental club run the most successful recycling program in the state? Then explain what you did so other groups can learn from your success.

Did something go wrong with your marketing plan and cause problems elsewhere? Use that cause-and-effect relationship to organize your speech.

Was your nonprofit able to reduce its gasoline costs this year? Tell what caused that improvement: better maintenance, more efficient routes, wiser use of electronic media (more Skype, less driving to meetings), etc.

NUMERICAL ORDER

You can go from the highest to the lowest number, or from the lowest to the highest.

Suppose you want to show how your volume of oil production has increased. Look at the numbers as part of an escalating trend. Relate them to specific events so the audience can see *why* your oil production went up.

Suppose you want to show how theft has been reduced in your distribution department. Explain to your audience *why* those numbers went down.

Always relate numbers to *human* events. That's the only way they will make sense to your audience.

PROBLEM-SOLUTION APPROACH

Is there something wrong with your tuition aid program? Then tell your audience about the problem and propose some solutions.

Do this with candor and honesty. If you have a problem, bring it out into the open. Chances are, your audience *already* knows about the problem. Admit it honestly, and you'll come across as credible.

Also, if you think your proposed solutions will be difficult, say so. No one likes a snow job.

GEOGRAPHICAL ORDER

Organizing a national sales conference? Start by reporting sales in the eastern districts and work west.

Reviewing the physical expenditures of your company's plants? Start with the northern ones and work south.

Evaluating the productivity of your bank's branches? Take it neighborhood by neighborhood.

Organizing a Global Town Hall for the 8,000 employees of your corporation? Greet your employees country by country—preferably, in the language of that country: *"Guten Tag," "Bonjour,"* and around the globe.

ALPHABETICAL ORDER

Why not? This certainly is easy for the audience to follow. And there are times when alphabetical order may be the only way to organize your information—lists of committees or departments, for example.

PSYCHOLOGICAL ORDER

Sometimes it's best to organize your speech based on the psychological needs of the audience.

What will they find most acceptable? Most comfortable? Most interesting? Put that first.

Think about the attitudes your audience may have. If you expect them to be hostile or resistant, then ease slowly into your speech. Begin on common ground and put your most acceptable ideas up front.

Don't expect to convince everyone of everything. There's usually a limit to the controversial ideas that any audience can accept.

Some sensitive areas in the business world (pro/antinuclear

power and labor/management confrontations, for example) *require* attention to psychological order.

TRANSITIONS

No matter which method you use, make sure you follow the order smoothly. *Do not jump from one topic to another.* Do not get sidetracked.

If you say something like, "But before I do that, I'd like to give you a little background on the history of our firm," you're heading for trouble.

Keep things moving. Use strong transitions to help the audience follow your ideas. Try such transitional phrases as:

- Moving on to the second territory . . .
- Now let's look at . . .
- So much for supply, but what about demand?
- Switching now to the western division . . .
- Looking ahead to the next five years . . .

Think of these transitions as verbal "signals" that will help the audience keep on track.

President Harry Truman did an outstanding job of using a verbal signal to underscore this main point in 1951: "In the simplest terms, what we are doing in Korea is this: We are trying to prevent a Third World War."

SPECIAL CIRCUMSTANCES

Your company faces a serious crisis, and it's your job to explain the issue to the employees.

1. Present several undeniable facts that show the seriousness of the situation. Do this *up front.* Be sure to do it without exaggeration, or the audience will suspect your motives.

2. Explore possible solutions to the crisis: tighter budget control, increased productivity, etc.

3. Solicit the ideas and support of *everyone* in the company to make the program work. Let them know exactly what you expect from them.

Caution:
Don't treat every situation like a crisis, or you will lose credibility. You are entitled to one, maybe two, crises in your career. No more.

If you try to turn every situation into a crisis, your audience will see you as the child who cried wolf once too often. They won't bother to listen anymore.

How to admit you've made a mistake
Have you shown an error in judgment? Made a foolish decision? Chosen the wrong person for a job? Backed the losing team? Pursued a dangerous course?

No sense in hiding your role. Everyone already knows. So, bring your mistake out in the open, clear the air, and set the stage to move on.

How to handle an emotional moment
Dealing with a tragedy? A community crisis? A natural disaster? Be realistic. The audience is likely exhausted, sad, scared, angry, and/or frustrated. They have neither the time nor the inclination to listen to long speeches.

Your own emotions may well overcome you, so it's wise to think about how you might handle yourself *before* you begin speaking in any emotionally charged situation.

In his remarks following the devastation of Hurricane Sandy, New Jersey governor Chris Christie stood side-by-side with President Obama, projecting strength as he urged the residents of his state to move forward:

> What I said yesterday I really mean. I know there has got to be sorrow . . . And that sorrow is appropriate; we've suffered some loss. Luckily, we haven't suffered that much loss of life and we thank God for that. But we have suffered losses, and this is the worst storm I've seen in my lifetime in this state. But we cannot permit that sorrow to replace the resilience that I know all New Jerseyans have. And so we will get up and we'll get this thing rebuilt, and we'll put things back together, because that's what this state is all about.

How to express disappointment

Suppose some big plan failed—and failed publicly. Now it's your responsibility to tell the audience why the old plan failed and to make some new proposals.

Beware: The audience may be extremely sensitive about the issue and they may fear being blamed for the whole mess. Reassure them that the original plan was a good one. Say it made sense based on the information available at the time it was conceived. Say no one could have predicted the sudden changes in events that caused the original plan to fail.

Once the audience feels safe from any finger-pointing, they will be receptive to your message. State the problem clearly and objectively. Admit disappointment, but don't dwell on past failures. Let your emphasis be on a new plan that's based on new data.

How to turn a negative into a positive

An example:

While historic preservation is a key part of both economic and environmental trends, its value is often overlooked. Too many people look at a worn-out old building and just see . . . well, they just see a worn-out old building. Enter New Hampshire Senator Jeanie Forrester.

Senator Forrester gave the welcoming remarks at the New Hampshire Preservation Alliance Conference in March 2013. How did she get the audience (and the media) to appreciate the often overlooked work that is accomplished by preservation societies every day? She used this great line:

> Some people can look at a building and say, "I built that." But preservationists like you have a slightly different take. You can point to a worn-out structure and tell everyone with pride, "I saved that."

Notice how Senator Forrester used first-person comments: "I built that" and "I saved that." This technique makes any speech more interesting and more persuasive.

One final point

Check your speech to make sure that if you say "first," you follow it with a "second." Otherwise your audience—and maybe even you—will become hopelessly lost.

Be careful not to use more than one set of "first, second, third" references. Used more than once per speech, this technique is confusing.

TELL THEM WHAT YOU TOLD THEM: THE CONCLUSION

Now's the time to sum it up—simply and directly. No new thoughts, please. You must avoid the temptation to stick in any additional points at the end. It's too late for that. Your conclusion may be the only thing the audience remembers, so make it memorable.

Here are some effective ways to end a speech:

EXPRESS APPRECIATION

In her New Year's remarks for 2013, German chancellor Angela Merkel closed with this expression of gratitude:

> At this hour in particular we should think about those who ensure our security, both here at home and far away.
>
> They are our soldiers, police officers, and civilian helpers who do their job for us at great personal sacrifice. I know from my conversations with them, how much it means to them when we at home think of them. I especially want to express my thanks to them tonight.
>
> . . . Together, let us make the New Year one in which we again put our greatest strengths to the test: our togetherness, our continued capacity for new ideas that gives us economic power. Then Germany will continue to be compassionate and successful. . . .

SHARE YOUR PERSONAL PHILOSOPHY

When Harvey Mackay, bestselling author of *Swim With the Sharks Without Being Eaten Alive,* gave the MBA commencement address at Penn State University, he created a strong emotional appeal by sharing this story from his boyhood:

> When I was a kid, my father knew a guy named Bernie who had started out his career with a vegetable stand, worked hard all his life, and eventually became wealthy as a fruit and vegetable wholesaler.

Every summer, when the first good watermelons came in, Dad would take me down to Bernie's warehouse and we'd have a feast. Bernie would choose a couple of watermelons just in from the field, crack them open, and hand each of us a big piece. Then, with Bernie taking the lead, we'd eat only the heart of the watermelon—the reddest, juiciest, most perfect part—and throw the rest away.

My father never made a lot of money. We were raised to clean our plates and not waste food. Bernie was my father's idea of a rich man. I always thought it was because he'd been such a success in business.

It was years before I realized my father admired Bernie's "richness" because he knew how to stop work in the middle of a summer day, sit down with his friends, and spend time eating the heart of the watermelon.

Being rich isn't about money. Being rich is a state of mind. Some of us, no matter how much money we have, will never be free enough to take the time to stop and eat the heart of the watermelon. And some of us will be rich without ever being more than a paycheck ahead of the game. . . .

END WITH A VERSE OF SCRIPTURE

For eulogies and memorial tributes, a Biblical verse might create the calming tone you wish to use with a grieving audience. Here is how President Barack Obama ended his speech at the interfaith vigil in Newtown, Connecticut, in honor of the victims of the shootings at Sandy Hill Elementary:

"Let the little children come to me," Jesus said, "and do not hinder them—for to such belongs the kingdom of heaven."
Charlotte. Daniel. Olivia. Josephine. Ana. Dylan. Madeleine. Catherine. Chase. Jesse. James. Grace. Emilie. Jack. Noah. Caroline. Jessica. Benjamin. Avielle. Allison.

God has called them all home. For those of us who remain, let us find the strength to carry on, and make our country worthy of their memory.

May God bless and keep those we've lost in His heavenly place. May He grace those we still have with His holy comfort. And may He bless and watch over this community, and the United States of America.

END WITH ACTIVE VERBS

Remember grammar class? Remember the parts of speech—verbs, nouns, adjectives, adverbs? Well, in speechwriting, verbs rank at the top. Make your verbs strong and active. The shorter and stronger the verb, the better the speaker's delivery.

Some examples of strong verbs:

- President Lyndon B. Johnson, in a radio speech during the riots of the '60s: "There is no American right to loot stores, or to burn buildings, or to fire rifles from the rooftops." Note the short verbs he used, all four-letter, all one-syllable: loot, burn, fire.

- President Woodrow Wilson, at a speech in Washington, DC: "Every man who takes office in Washington either grows or swells . . . I watch him carefully to see whether he is swelling or growing." Again, note the power of one-syllable verbs: grows, swells.

- Her Majesty Queen Beatrix of the Netherlands, on the occasion of her 2013 state visit to Singapore, chose a distinctive verb: "Singapore buzzes with energy!" Also note the power of a mere four-word sentence.

END WITH A STRONG RHETORICAL QUESTION

Something like this can be effective: "Can we afford to do it? A more relevant question is, can we afford *not* to?"

END WITH WORDS THAT *SOUND* STRONG

- "We need to return to that old-fashioned notion of competition—where *substance,* not *subsidies,* determines the winner." This ending focuses the audience's attention on two contrasting words that begin with the same syllable—*sub.*

- "We worked hard to get this department in tip-top shape. We plan to keep it that way." *Tip-top* repeats the opening and closing consonant sounds.

- "Yes, we ran into some problems, but we corrected them. Perhaps our message should be 'Sighted sub, sank same.'" Good use of alliteration—the repetition of initial consonant sounds.

- "Our personnel department's training program works on the premise that 'earning' naturally follows 'learning.'" Rhyme can be catchy, but use it judiciously.

END WITH A STRONG COMMITMENT

At the National Day of Prayer and Remembrance following the 9/11 terrorist attacks, Vice Admiral Thad Allen, U.S. Coast Guard, concluded his remarks at Norfolk Virginia Waterside Park this way:

We cannot explain the unexplainable. We cannot change the past. We cannot restore what is lost.

But we can be here, and we can say to those who are suffering: We believe . . .

We live by our core values of honor, respect and devotion to duty. We *honor* those who died. We *respect* our law and authorities. We remain *devoted to duty* whatever that duty is, and wherever that duty may take us.

We will be *Semper Paratus* . . . Always Ready.

SIX

HOW TO MAKE IT SIMPLE

*The most valuable of all talents is that of never
using two words when one will do.*
—THOMAS JEFFERSON

HOW TO MAKE EVERY WORD COUNT

Speeches are meant to be heard, not read. That means you have to keep your language simple and easily understood. Write for the ear, not the eye.

Remember: Your audience will have only one shot to get your message. They can't go back and reread a section that's fuzzy, as they can with a book or a newspaper article. Get rid of any fuzzy parts *before* you give the speech.

Never be content with your first draft. *Never.* After you've written it, read it aloud.

Let some time elapse between your rewrites. Let the whole thing sit overnight or over a couple of nights, if possible. Then go at it with a red pen. Use your delete button. Cut ruthlessly.

This chapter will show you—in step-by-step detail—how to simplify the language in your speech. It will help you:

- choose the right words

- simplify your phrases

- sharpen your sentences

USE SIMPLE, DIRECT WORDS

Use the following list to make your own substitutions:

Instead of	Try using
abbreviate	shorten
accommodate	serve
advise	tell
aggregate	total, whole
anticipate	expect
approximately	about
ascertain	find out, figure out
burgeoning	growing
cessation	end
cognizant	aware
commencement	start, beginning
compel	make
component	part
conjecture	guess
currently	now
deceased	dead
demonstrate	show
desire	want
determine	find out
diminutive	little
discourse	talk
disseminate	spread
duplicate	copy
eliminate	cut out
elucidate	clarify
encounter	meet
endeavor	try
engage	hire
eradicate	wipe out

Instead of	Try using
execute	do
expedite	speed
expire	die
facilitate	make easy
feasible	send
forward	send
generate	make, cause
heretofore	until now
illustrate	show
indicate	say
initial	first
inquire	ask
locate	find
maintenance	upkeep
marginal	small
numerous	many
observe	see, watch
obtain	get
operate	work, use
originated	began
peruse	read
precipitate	cause
presently	soon
procure	get, take
recapitulate	sum up
recess	break
remunerate	pay
render	give, send
represents	is
require	need
reside	live
residence	home

Instead of	Try using
retain	keep
review	check
saturate	soak
solicit	ask
stated	said
stringent	strict
submit	send
subsequent	next
substantial	large
sufficient	enough
supply	send
terminate	end
utilize	use
vacate	leave
vehicle	truck, car, van, bus
verification	proof

A final point: The Gettysburg Address is one of the world's most memorable speeches. Lincoln wrote 76 percent of it with words *of five letters or less*. Consider that an inspiration for you to do the same.

AVOID JARGON

Infrastructure is the longest word any of us in politics have learned to say, so we say it a lot.
        —CAROL BELLAMY, FORMER
    NEW YORK CITY COUNCIL PRESIDENT

Jargon doesn't work in a speech. It smacks of bureaucratese and audiences tend to block it out. It may even alienate some listeners. Get rid of it.

Jargon	Plain English
a guesstimate	a rough estimate
conceptualize	imagine
finalize	finish, complete
implement	carry out
interface (verb)	talk with
meaningful	real
operational	okay, working
optimum	best
output	results
parameters	limits
utilization	use
viable	workable

AVOID EUPHEMISMS

Euphemisms bloat a speech. Replace them with plain English.

Euphemism	Plain English
classification device	test
disadvantaged	poor
inventory shrinkage	theft
motivational deprivation	laziness
passed away	died
terminated	fired
unlawful or arbitrary deprivation of life	murder
unscheduled intensified repairs	emergency repairs

AVOID VAGUE MODIFIERS

Words such as "very," "slightly," and "extremely" are too vague to be useful. Use words or phrases that say *precisely* what you mean.

Vague:
The personnel department is rather understaffed, but the situation will be corrected in the very near future.

Specific:
The personnel department has three vacancies. We will fill these jobs within the next month.

DON'T SPEAK IN ABBREVIATIONS

You may know what SEC and FCC stand for, but don't assume that everyone else does.

You have to explain every abbreviation you use—not *every* time you use it, but at least the *first* time.

The same goes with acronyms, such as NOW (National Organization for Women) and PAC (political action committee). Unlike those abbreviations that are pronounced letter by letter (SEC, FCC, for example), acronyms are pronounced like words. You can use them in a speech, but be sure to identify them the first time.

This is a particular problem in the military, where abbreviations and acronyms are regularly sprinkled throughout written communications—and often creep into oral presentations, as well.

While other military folks might understand your abbreviations, the public at large finds them peculiar, even off-putting.

Root them out of your public presentations. You'll reach a lot more minds, persuade a lot more people, and make a lot more friends. Isn't that why you're speaking in the first place?

DON'T SPEAK IN UNFAMILIAR LANGUAGES

Every four years, the U.S. presidential election brings a fresh crop of candidates, some of whom try to court voters by speaking in the foreign language of a particular neighborhood. Mostly this involves speakers butchering Spanish or Korean or Polish or some other language in their attempt to win votes.

Note to political candidates: If you have strong Spanish skills, wonderful. Use your Spanish. But if you're merely trying to throw in some foreign phrases to impress the audience, spare everyone. Stick with English rather than embarrass yourself or insult the intelligence of your audience.

On the other hand, *if you were born or reared in a foreign country,* you may use your native language to great effect.

Find an appropriate proverb from your native country . . . work it into your speech . . . offer it to the audience in your native tongue . . . pause . . . then give the English translation.

This well-timed delivery can greatly increase audience interest and help build emotional appeal. When Jeffrey Steiner, as chairman and CEO of the Fairchild Corporation, spoke in 1992 on the five hundredth anniversary of the arrival of Jews in Turkey, he included a Yiddish proverb:

When Sephardic Jews were expelled from Spain, they found a safe haven in Turkey. And, for half a millennium, Turkey has continued to extend a special benevolence to Jewish people fleeing persecution.

I know. I was one of those people. During World War II, my family sought refuge in Turkey. We were able to escape the Nazis, and flee Vienna, and find safety in Istanbul. . . .

The history of the Jewish community in Turkey is remarkable.

There is a Yiddish proverb that fits the spirit of our shared history: *"A barg mit a barg kumt zikh nit tsunoyf, ober a mentsh mit a mentshn yo."* Translation: "Two mountains can't come together, but two people can."

You see, for half a millennium, the republic of Turkey has proven that men and women of good will *can* meet . . . that tolerance and respect *can* cross the "mountains" of geographic borders . . . that people of different faiths *can* live together in harmony.

Note: Senator John Kerry used this technique in his 2004 campaign for the U.S. presidency. Kerry's wife was Hispanic, he was comfortable speaking the language, and he effectively used Spanish when campaigning in Spanish-speaking areas. In 2013, as U.S. Secretary of State, Kerry spoke French in his opening remarks at a joint press conference with the French foreign minister. (Kerry had learned French while attending a Swiss boarding school.) The French were delighted by Kerry's gesture, with news headlines touting: "Le numéro de charme en français de John Kerry."

AVOID SEXIST LANGUAGE

There are several good ways to avoid sexist implications in your speech.

Find substitutes for compound nouns that contain man or woman
This list should help.

businessmen	businesspeople
cleaning woman	office cleaner
congressmen	members of Congress
firemen	firefighters
foreman	supervisor
housewife	homemaker

insurance salesman	insurance agent
mailmen	mail carriers
man-hours	worker-hours
mankind	human beings
manpower	labor force
man's achievements	human achievements
policemen	police officer
political man	political behavior
repairman	repairperson/service rep
salesman	sales reps, sales clerks, sales force
spokesman	spokesperson
statesman	leader
stewardess	flight attendant

Shift to the plural

Before:

When a *manager* goes on a business trip, *he* should save all of *his* receipts.

After:

When *managers* go on business trips, *they* should save all of *their* receipts.

Restructure the sentence

Before:

The company will select someone from the Treasury Department to be chairman of the Travel and Entertainment Committee.

After:

The company will select someone from the Treasury Department to head the Travel and Entertainment Committee.

Alternate male and female examples

Before:

Interviewers are too quick to say, *"He* doesn't have enough technical knowledge," or *"He's* just not the right *man* for us."

After:

Interviewers are too quick to say, *"He* doesn't have enough technical knowledge," or *"She's* just not the right *person* for us."

Be sure that you don't always mention the male first. Switch the order: husbands and wives, hers or his, him or her, women and men.

SIMPLIFY YOUR PHRASES

Everything should be made as simple as possible,
but not simpler.

—ALBERT EINSTEIN

A phrase with too many words becomes meaningless. Look at your draft, and get rid of pompous, wordy, and overwritten constructions. Use the following list as a guideline:

Instead of	Try using
a large number of	many
a sufficient number of	enough
a total of 42	42
advance planning	planning
are in agreement with	agree with
as indicated in the the following chart	the chart shows
as you know	*Delete* (if they already know, why tell them?)
at that point in time	then
at the present time	now
at the time of presenting	now

Instead of	Try using
this speech	today
basically unaware of	did not know
be that as it may	but
blame it on	blame
both alike	alike
brief in duration	short
bring the matter to the attention of	tell
caused damage to	damaged
check into the facts	check the facts
consensus of opinion	consensus
continue on	continue
curiously enough	curiously
demonstrates the ability to	can
despite the fact that	although
due to the fact that	because
end product	product
equally as	equally
estimated at about	estimated at
exert a leadership role	lead
firm commitment	commitment
for free	free
for the purpose of	for
frame of reference	viewpoint, perspective
give encouragement to	encourage
have a discussion	discuss
hold a meeting	meet
hold in abeyance	suspend
in close proximity	near
in connection with	on, of
individuals who will participate	participants
in many cases	often

Instead of	Try using
in order to	to
in some cases	sometimes
in the area of	approximately
in the course of	during
in the event of	if
in the majority of instances	most often, usually
in the vicinity of	near
in view of	because
is equipped with	has
is in an operational state	operates, works
is noted to have	has
is of the opinion that	thinks
it has been shown that	*Delete*
it is recognized that	*Delete*
it is recommended by me that	I recommend
it may be mentioned that	*Delete*
join together	join
made a complete reversal	reversed
make a decision	decide
my personal opinion	my opinion
needless to say	*Delete*
never before in the past	never
new innovations	innovations
newly created	new
obtain an estimate	estimate
off of	off
of sufficient magnitude	big enough
on a national basis	nationally
on the basis of	from
on the occasion of	when
optimum utilization	best use
over with	over

Instead of	Try using
past experience	experience
personal friend	friend
predicated on	based on
prior to	before
provide assistance to	help
start off	start
study in depth	study
subsequent to	after
take action	act
the major portion	most
the reason why is that	because
until such time as	until
very unique	unique
was in communication with	talked with
with reference to	about
with regard to	about
with the exception of	except
with the result that	so that
would invoke an expenditure of approximately	would cost about

AVOID THE FLUFF PITFALL

If your speech is filled with statements such as, "This has been a most challenging year," or "We all face a golden opportunity," or "We will meet our challenges with optimism and view our future with confidence," it is probably high on fluff and low on content. Unfortunately, too many business speeches fall into this category.

Try this experiment: Listen to ten ordinary business speeches and count the number of times words such as "challenge" and "opportunity" are used. Pay careful attention to the opening and closing sections of the speeches, because that's where inexperienced speakers tend to use the most generalities.

Then, listen to ten speeches that you can assume to be ghostwritten—speeches, for example, that are given by a top CEO or by the U.S. president. These speeches will have fewer "challenges" and "opportunities" in their texts. Why? Because professional speechwriters know better. Professional speechwriters know audiences just block this airy stuff out.

Follow the professionals. Review your speech and get rid of glib expressions. If you want your message to stand out, put content—not fluff—into your speech.

SHARPEN YOUR SENTENCES

When "whom" is correct, recast the sentence.
                                        —WILLIAM SAFIRE

There are several important things to know about sentences.

PUT TIME REFERENCES AT THE BEGINNING OF SENTENCES

Let the audience hear your time frame first. Say, "Since 2013, we have _____." Don't say, "We have _____ since 2013."

This technique improves audience comprehension. It's also easier for a speaker to deliver. (*A quick exercise:* Try it both ways. Read both versions aloud. You'll hear the difference.)

PUT PLACE REFERENCES AT THE BEGINNING OF SENTENCES

Let the audience hear the geography before you provide other details. Say, "Throughout Taiwan, we have created _____," not "We have created _____ throughout Taiwan."

Again, citing the location upfront makes it easier for an audience to follow your message.

SHORT SENTENCES ARE STRONGER THAN LONG SENTENCES

Try this experiment: Take a sample page from your draft and count the number of words in each sentence. Write the numbers down and average them.

If you average twenty or more words per sentence, you'd better start cutting. Why? Because an audience can't follow what you're saying if you put too many words in a sentence. Your message just gets lost.

If you don't believe me, read your longest sentence aloud, then read your shortest sentence aloud. See which one is more powerful—and more memorable.

VARIETY IS THE SPICE OF LIFE

If all your sentences are long, no one will be able to follow you. But if all your sentences are short, your speech may become boring. People get tired of hearing the same rhythm. If you use a rather long sentence, precede or follow it with a short, punchy one. The contrast will catch your audience's attention.

FDR was a master of this technique, and his speeches show a great sense of rhythm and timing. Consider the following example. He uses a powerful, two-word sentence followed by a rhythmic, eighteen-word sentence:

Hostilities exist. There is no mincing the fact that our people, our territory, and our interests are in grave danger.

Ronald Reagan also knew how to vary the rhythm of his speech:

Everyone is against protectionism in the abstract. That is easy. It is another matter to make the hard, courageous choices when it is your industry or your business that appears to be hurt by foreign competition. I know. We in the United States deal with the problem of protectionism every day of the year.

Count the words he used: seven in the first sentence, then three, then twenty-six, then two, then sixteen. Average length? About eleven words per sentence.

USE THE ACTIVE, NOT THE PASSIVE, VOICE

It's time for a grammar lesson. I'll keep it brief.

The following sentences are in the *active voice* because they show that the subject acts, or does something:

- The Customer Inquiry Department *answers* almost four hundred phone calls every day.

- Our new maintenance program *saved* the company $5,000 in the first six months.

- The committee *records* all suggestions in a logbook.

- Government *must place* some constraints on these contracts to prevent price excesses.

A sentence is in the *passive voice* when the subject is acted upon:

- Almost four hundred phone calls *are answered* by the Customer Inquiry Department every day.

- Five thousand dollars *was saved* by the company in the first six months of our new maintenance program.

- All suggestions *are recorded* by the committee in a logbook.

- Some constraints *must be placed* on these contracts by government to prevent price excesses.

Read the above sentences aloud, and notice that the active voice:

1. sounds more vigorous
2. sounds more personal
3. uses fewer words
4. is easier to follow
5. is easier to remember

Get rid of passive constructions in your speech. They sound stilted, flat, and contrived.

LIMIT THE NUMBER OF ADJECTIVES

Nouns and verbs are almost pure metal; adjectives are cheaper ore.

–MARIE GILCHRIST

Try this test: Pick any two-to-three-page segment of your speech manuscript and underline the adjectives. Now, delete some of those adjectives—read the section out loud—and see if your speech-writing sounds crisper and stronger. If you really need those adjectives, fine, put them back in. If not? Just leave them out.

CUT ADVERBS

In my upper-level speechwriting seminars, I urge the speechwriters to try this experiment: Cut all the adverbs on any given page. Ask yourself, "Do I honestly need to put those adverbs back in?" Most of the time, adverbs just "pad" a speech. Cut them. Then read the page aloud, and listen. You'll probably find the message becomes stronger when you take away those adverbs.

Remember: A strong manuscript helps ensure a strong delivery.

The more adverbs in a speech, the more contrived that speech will sound. Consider:

"We carefully deliberated . . ." vs "We deliberated . . ."

"I thoughtfully reflected on . . ." vs "I reflected on . . ."

"He hastily escaped . . ." vs "He escaped."

We tend not to use adverbs in ordinary, everyday conversation. Why use them in a presentation?

CUT "I THINK," "I BELIEVE," "I KNOW," "IT SEEMS TO ME THAT," "IN MY OPINION"

These expressions weaken sentences. Cut them, and you will make your sentences stronger.

Before:
We think prices are already too high and I believe people are hurting.

After:
Prices are already too high and people are hurting.

AVOID "THERE ARE"

Sentences that begin with "There are . . ." are often weak. Try rewriting them.

Before:
There are alternative ways that must be found by us to solve the problem.

After:
We must find alternative ways to solve the problem.

BEWARE OF TONGUE TWISTERS

Read your speech aloud several times, and listen carefully for potential tongue twisters, especially those that might come out sounding obscene. Consider this 1988 gaffe by former president George H. W. Bush:

"For seven and a half years I've worked alongside President Reagan. We've had triumphs. Made some mistakes. We've had some sex . . . uh . . . setbacks." [Note: It can be hard to say multiple words beginning with "s" . . . as the former president learned the hard way. Rewrite anything that might create a glitch for you.]

When I coach speakers, I tell them, "If you trip over a word in a practice session, that probably means we should rewrite the sentence."

IN SHORT, CUT AS MUCH AS POSSIBLE

The writer Thomas Wolfe tended to overwrite his early drafts—producing in such a huge quantity that he had to deliver his manuscripts to the publisher in a trunk. I can only imagine what his editor, the esteemed Maxwell Perkins, must have thought upon receiving manuscripts so bulky they could only be delivered in a trunk.

But I can tell you this: Speakers who give their audiences over-long presentations will flat-out lose their audiences. Listeners fortunate enough to sit on the aisle or at the back of the auditorium will simply stand up and walk out. Those poor folks stuck in the middle of the room might not be able to leave physically, but they'll leave mentally: texting friends, making grocery lists, or just plain dozing. Either way, a too-long speech will lose its audience.

So, cut. As much as possible.

A QUICK SUMMATION

In his essay "Politics and the English Language," George Orwell tells how to make your writing simple:

1. Never use a long word where a short one will do.
2. If it is possible to cut a word out, always cut it out.
3. Never use the passive where you can use the active.
4. Never use a foreign phrase, a scientific word, or a jargon word if you can think of an everyday English equivalent.
5. Break any of these rules sooner than say anything barbarous.

THE ULTIMATE TEST

David Belasco, the great American theatrical producer, once said, "If you can't write your idea on the back of my calling card, you don't have a clear idea."

So, get out your business card, and see if you can put your main idea on the card. If it fits, wonderful. If not, maybe your idea is too flabby. Whittle. Cut.

SEVEN

STYLE

Poetry has everything to do with speeches—cadence, rhythm, imagery, sweep, a knowledge that words are magic, that words like children have the power to make dance the dullest beanbag of a heart.
—PEGGY NOONAN

Business owners, politicians, nonprofit leaders, corporate executives, military professionals, medical professionals, fund-raisers, community activists, entrepreneurs, and educators give thousands of speeches every day. Most of these speeches are forgotten as soon as the audience leaves the room—if not sooner.

But some speeches *do* linger in the minds and hearts of audiences. What makes these speeches special? Style.

Speeches with style have a certain "ring" that makes them *easy* to remember. They have a psychological appeal that makes them seem *important* to remember. And they create an impact that makes them irresistibly *quotable*.

Here are some techniques that professional speechwriters use.

HOW TO USE TRIPARTITE DIVISION

Tripartite division is a device that breaks things into three parts. Three has always been a powerful number. Consider:

- the Holy Trinity

- the three wise men and their three gifts

- in children's literature: *Goldilocks and the Three Bears, The Three Little Pigs,* and *The Three Little Kittens*

- in baseball: Three strikes and you're out!

- from the battlefield: Ready! Aim! Fire!

The human mind is strongly attracted to things that come in "three's." Throughout history, speakers have used tripartite division as a powerful rhetorical device.

- *Julius Caesar:* "Veni, vidi, vici." ("I came, I saw, I conquered.")

- *Abraham Lincoln:* "We cannot dedicate, we cannot consecrate, we cannot hallow this ground."

- *Douglas MacArthur's farewell address at West Point:* "Duty, honor, country: Those three hallowed words reverently dictate what you ought to be, what you can be, what you will be."

- *President Harry S. Truman, in a special message to Congress:* "America was built on courage, on imagination, and an unbeatable determination to do the job at hand."

- *President Reagan, in Normandy, on the fortieth anniversary of D-Day:* "The Soviet troops that came to the center of this continent did not leave when peace came. They are still there— uninvited, unwanted, unyielding, almost forty years after the war."

- *Jimmy Carter, in his Farewell Address:* "We see our earth as it really is—a small and fragile and beautiful globe, the only home we have." [Notice how he built his triad from using words that went from short to long: "small," one syllable; "fragile," two syllables; "beautiful," four syllables.]

- *Coast Guard Commandant Admiral Robert J. Papp's 2013 leadership address:* "We continue to watch the creation of a new ocean in the arctic, and the traffic and commercial activity and tourism that come with it . . . But as human activity increases, so must our presence. We have the authorities, the responsibility, and an obligation to be there."

- *Honorable Michael B. Donley, Secretary of the Air Force, in September 2012, to the Air Force Association Air and Space Conference:* ". . . the men and women of the United States Air Force continue to provide unmatched *Global Vigilance, Global Reach*, and *Global Power* across the full spectrum of operations."

- *Secretary of State Hillary Clinton* spoke about "the three D's" of national security: an easy way to remember her three tenants of diplomacy, development, and defense.

Admittedly these are well-known speakers from the pages of history, but everyone can make tripartite division work to their advantage.

- *A civic leader:* "The promise is there, the logic is overwhelming, the need is great."

- *The recipient of an award for community service:* "My volunteer work has been my life, my inspiration, my joy."

- *A bank manager:* "We do not wield the power we once did—power over our employees, our customers, our communities."

Triads are an easy way to add style to oral communication.

When Pennsylvania governor Tom Ridge unveiled newly minted commemorative quarters in a ceremony at the U.S. Mint in Philadelphia, he used these triads:

> Pennsylvania quarters aren't just quarters—they're tiny, silver reminders of Pennsylvania's past, Pennsylvania's pride, and Pennsylvania's promise. They tell our story, symbolize our heritage, and add to our legacy—all for twenty-five cents.

On Palm Sunday 2013, leading his first major service since election to the papacy, Pope Francis expressed his theme in the form of a triad when he spoke about our need to help "the humble, the poor, the forgotten." Then, departing from his prepared manuscript for a moment to refer to wealth, he used the folk wisdom of his grandmother: "You can't take it with you, my grandmother used to say."

HOW TO USE PARALLELISM

Use a parallel structure to create balance—the emotional appeal of harmony.

- *John Fitzgerald Kennedy:* "If a free society cannot help the many who are poor, it cannot save the few who are rich."

- *Richard Nixon:* "Where peace is unknown, make it welcome; where peace is fragile, make it strong; where peace is temporary, make it permanent."

In a state of the union address, President Lyndon Johnson drew attention with these words: "Thomas Jefferson said no nation can be both ignorant and free. Today, no nation can be both ignorant and great."

HOW TO USE IMAGERY

Be specific, be vivid, be colorful—and you will make your point.
Even better, your audience will *remember* your point.

- *Winston Churchill:* "An iron curtain has descended across the Continent."

- *Herbert Hoover:* "We do not need to burn down the house to kill the rats."

- *Franklin Delano Roosevelt:* "When you see a rattlesnake poised to strike, you do not wait until he has struck before you crush him."

- *John F. Kennedy, First Inaugural address:* "In the past, those who foolishly sought power by riding the back of the tiger ended up inside." [Note: Tiger imagery has distinguished many historic speeches. Consider FDR: "No man can tame a tiger into a kitten by stroking it."]

- *George H. W. Bush:* "The American symbol is an eagle, not an ostrich—and now is not the time to go burying our heads in the sand."

HOW TO USE INVERSION OF ELEMENTS

If you switch the elements in paired statements, you can produce some memorable lines.

- *John Fitzgerald Kennedy:* "Ask not what your country can do for you. Ask what you can do for your country."

A quick exercise:
See how these speakers changed just one word in a key phrase to build interest and create quotable lines.

- *Franklin D. Roosevelt, Second Inaugural address:* "We have always known that heedless self-interest was bad morals; we know now that it is bad economics."

- *Lyndon B. Johnson, speech at the University of Michigan:* "The Great Society . . . is a place where men are more concerned with the quality of their goals than the quantity of their goods."

HOW TO USE REPETITION

Audiences do not always pay attention. Their minds wander. They think about the work that's piled up on their desks. They think about the bills that are piled up at home. They often miss whole sections of a speech.

If you have an important word, phrase, sentence, or structure, be sure to repeat it—again and again.

When H. Norman Schwarzkopf, hero of Operation Desert Storm, returned to the United States to deliver an address before the Joint Session of Congress, he used repetition to drive home a point with enormous power and pride:

> We were all volunteers and we were regulars. We were Reservists and we were National Guardsmen, serving side-by-side as we have in every war, because that's what the U.S. military is.
>
> And we were men and women, each of us bearing our fair share of the load and none of us quitting because the conditions were too rough or the job was too tough, because that's what your military is.
>
> We were black and white and yellow and brown and red, and we noticed when our blood was shed in the desert it didn't separate by race but it flowed together, because that's what your military is. . . .

Former secretary of state Condoleezza Rice emphasized the message by repeating a key phrase in her speech to the 2012 Republican National Convention:

> I can remember as if it were yesterday when my young assistants came into my office at the White House to say that a plane had hit the World Trade Center, and then a second plane, and then a third plane, the Pentagon. And later, we would learn that a plane had crashed into a field in Pennsylvania, driven into the ground by brave souls who died so that others might live.
>
> From that day on—from that day on, our sense of vulnerability and our concepts of security were never the same again.

A quick exercise:
Read aloud the following excerpt from Winston Churchill. Hear the full power of his repetition technique:

> . . . we shall fight in France, we shall fight on the seas and oceans, we shall fight with growing confidence and strength in the air, we shall defend our Island, whatever the cost may be, we shall fight on the beaches, we shall fight in the fields and in the streets, we shall fight in the hills; we shall never surrender . . .

HOW TO USE RHETORICAL QUESTIONS

Ask rhetorical questions to *involve* your audience. Pause a moment or so after each question. This will allow listeners some time to answer the question in their own minds—and it will help reinforce your message.

- *Grammy-winning singer k.d. lang, on behalf of animal rights:* "We all love animals, but why do we call some of them pets and some of them dinner?"

- *Bill Cosby, challenging the media's effect on children:* "The networks say they don't influence anybody. If that's true, why do they have commercials? Why am I sitting there with Jell-O pudding?"

HOW TO USE CONTRAST

Sharpen your point with contrasting words. Opposites pack a verbal punch—boosting audience comprehension and enhancing your delivery.

In his acceptance speech for the Republican nomination, Benjamin Harrison offered this comment about the service given by Union soldiers and sailors during the Civil War: "They gave ungrudgingly; it was not a trade, but an offering."

Richard Nixon, in a speech at the U.S. Air Force Academy in 1969, used imagery in this contrast: "The American defense establishment should never be a sacred cow, but on the other hand, the American military should never be anybody's scapegoat."

HOW TO USE RHYTHM

Cadence drives your message into the minds of the listeners.

When General Raymond Odierno spoke at the 2013 Medal of Honor Induction Ceremony of Staff Sgt. Clint Romesha, he ended with these rhythmic lines:

> Today, we honor Clint—a man of conviction and of courage. And by honoring him, we honor those heroes who fought so selflessly by his side, and all of our Soldiers who have raised their right hand to defend this country and defend our ideals. God bless all of you for coming today and God bless America. The strength of our Nation is our Army, the strength of our Army is our Soldiers, the strength of our Soldiers is our Families, and this is what makes us Army Strong!

HOW TO USE VIVID WORDS

We live now in hard times, not end times. And we
can have animus and not be enemies.
        —JON STEWART, RALLY TO RESTORE SANITY

Franklin Delano Roosevelt is forever identified with this memorable line about Pearl Harbor: "A date which will live in infamy."

"Infamy" is not a word we hear in everyday speeches. It jumps out.

Few people know, however, that the original draft of his speech read, "This is a day that will live in world history." FDR used the power of the pen (literally).

If you're hoping to generate media coverage for your speeches, vivid words can make all the difference. When I teach master-level seminars in speechwriting, I encourage the participants to make their speeches as "quotable" as possible—and wordplay does the trick.

Wordplay doesn't have to be complex. In fact, the best word-play is disarmingly simple. One quick change, one new syllable, and—voila! You have a quotable line.

When the FBI received criticism for taking too long to investigate the crash of TWA Flight 800, FBI Assistant Director James Kallstrom defended the lengthy probe: "We had to look at every dark crack and crevice in this investigation. We are the Federal Bureau of Total Investigation . . . not the Federal Bureau of the Obvious."

Create your own quotable phrases

- The chairman of the Federal Reserve, Ben Bernanke, coined the term "fiscal cliff" to describe the dire consequences looming unless elected officials would cooperate.

- In 2013, the Illinois Department of Public Health launched a campaign to celebrate the fifth anniversary of the Smoke-Free Illinois Act. And the phrase they coined to garner media attention for their initiative? "Thanks from the bottom of our lungs."

- Economist Jim O'Neill created the "BRIC" designation for the then-emerging economies of Brazil, Russia, India, and China.

- Eric Pooley, senior VP with the Environmental Defense Fund, addressed the topic of climate change with this memorable phrase: "Now, we have weather on steroids."

- New York Senator Charles Schumer said that if the U.S. tried to reduce gun violence without considering access to weapons and ammunition, that would be "like trying to prevent lung cancer without talking about cigarettes."

- Economist Albert Hirschman created popular use of the term "exit option."

- President of Finland Sauli Niinistö used this creative word-play when speaking at the Norwegian Institute on International Affairs: "The Arctic economy is not measured in quarters. The perspective is closer to a 'quarter of a century' than a 'quarter year.'"

- As secretary of state, Hillary Clinton visited more countries than any other secretary of state—logging close to a million travel miles in service to what she coined "economic statecraft."

EIGHT

HUMOR: WHAT WORKS,
WHAT DOESN'T, AND WHY

*Once you get people laughing, they're listening
and you can tell them almost anything.*
—HERBERT GARDNER

Some people think they absolutely must use a joke to begin a speech. I hope you are not one of these people.

Jokes can be risky. There's nothing worse than a joke that falls flat—unless it's a joke that falls flat at the beginning of a speech. Beware.

Ask yourself six questions before you plan to use humor *anywhere* in your speech:

- "Will this humor tie into the subject and mood of my speech?"

- "Will my audience feel comfortable with this humor?"

- "Is this story funny, short, and uncomplicated?"

- "Is this joke fresh?"

- "Can I be safe delivering this humor?" (If a journalist overheard it, if a blogger wrote about it, if your boss found out—would you worry about getting in trouble for it?)

- "Can I deliver this humor really well, with confidence and ease and perfect timing?"

If you can't answer "yes" to all of these questions, scrap the humor.

USE A LIGHT TOUCH

Professional comedians like jokes that produce loud laughs. But you are a speaker, not a professional comedian.

Don't focus on jokes that beg for loud laughs because this usually backfires. Instead, try to develop a "light touch" of humor. You can do this through:

- personal anecdotes
- one-liners that blend into the speech
- lighthearted stories from the day's news
- humorous quotations
- quips that seem off-the-cuff (but are actually planned)
- clever statistics
- wordplay
- gestures
- voice intonations
- raising an eyebrow
- pausing for an extra beat
- suddenly speeding up a particular line
- smiling

Using a light touch of humor will help the audience to see you as a decent, humane, and friendly person. It will help put the audience in a receptive mood for the message of your speech.

WHAT WORKS

What kind of humor works best in a speech? The kind that is friendly, personal, and natural. Humor in a speech doesn't need to produce guffaws. A few smiles and some chuckles are just fine for your purpose.

Where can you find this humor? Many speakers buy books of jokes and adapt the material to suit their own needs. Other speakers turn to the Internet to hire a comedy writer. I have to offer some cautions.

Purchased humor might be moderately helpful, but *only* if you use it judiciously.

Don't use purchased material verbatim. Always adapt the humor to your own needs and your own style. And always give it the sniff test. If the humor doesn't feel right, if it just doesn't "smell" right to you, don't use it. Period.

Why not learn to create *your own* light touches of humor? Original material will work better than jokes lifted straight from the Internet.

Why? Three big reasons:

1. If you create your own humorous touches, you can be sure this material will be fresh to your audience.

2. If the humor comes from your own experience, you will deliver it more naturally and more effectively.

3. If you share something personal with the audience, they will feel friendlier toward you.

It's not hard to create your own light touches. Your safest bet is to poke gentle fun at yourself. Try making light of:

- *Your fame.* A little boy once asked John F. Kennedy how he became a war hero. "It was absolutely involuntary," Kennedy replied. "They sank my boat."

- *Your origins.* Lyndon B. Johnson joked that, "A long time ago down in Texas I learned that telling a man to go to hell and making him go there are two different propositions."

- *Public perceptions of your work.* Connecticut politician Gloria Schaffer used this line: "Women's work is in the House and in the Senate."

- *Your observations.* New Hampshire senate president Peter Bragdon got laughs from this line in the 2012 election (debating whether out-of-state college students should be able to vote in NH or not): "I've heard of same-day registration, but not drive-by voting."

A CAUTION

Poking fun at yourself is the safest kind of humor, but never belittle your professional competence in your area of expertise. Otherwise, the audience will wonder why they should bother listening to you.

Never say anything about yourself that you might regret later. A speech is over in fifteen or twenty minutes, but a reputation lasts a lifetime. Don't sacrifice a reputation for a cheap laugh.

WHAT ARE YOUR CHANCES OF GETTING A LAUGH?

You'll find it's easier to get a laugh as the day goes on.

Think about it:

Early in the morning, people are still groggy. Their minds often aren't working well. If they think about anything at all, they think about the pile of work that lies ahead of them. They just want to have a cup of coffee and get moving with their schedule. They're not in a very playful mood—and it's hard to be funny when the audience doesn't want to play along.

So, if you're the guest speaker at a breakfast fund-raiser, for example, keep everything short and simple. Even if the audience is really interested in your cause, they will be anxious to get out of the meeting and get on with the day's work. No complicated jokes, please. A quick one-liner is probably all these people can handle.

By lunchtime, things ease up a bit. At least some of the day's work is done, and people can sit back and relax a little. Still, they have to get back to the office, and they will be looking at their watches if two o'clock approaches.

By dinnertime, things are as loose as they'll ever be. Work is over. People want to put their troubles behind them for a while. They're in the mood to unwind. Indulge them. Give them the chuckles they *want*.

By late evening, however, things may be *too* loose for humor to work. In fact, things may be too loose for *anything* to work—including the speaker! By ten or eleven o'clock, most audiences are either too inattentive, too inebriated, or too tired to be receptive to any message.

At this late hour, you must put aside your ego and put aside your prepared speech, no matter how witty or wise that speech might be.

Just give a three- or four-sentence capsule summary, flash a broad smile, and get out of there. The audience will love you for it.

A CAUTION ABOUT OUTDOOR EVENTS

Speaking outdoors? Be especially careful to keep your humor short.

At the opening of the Tip O'Neill Tunnel in Boston, Lt. Governor Kerry Healey drew a big laugh with this short quip:

The irony that we're naming a new portion of a roadway through the heart of Boston after Tip O'Neill would not be lost on him. Because as everyone in his family knows, but many people here may not: Tip was the world's worst driver!

Try this quick speechwriting exercise: Count the number of words in the above punch line (six), and the average number of letters per word in that punch line (just over four letters per word). That's short.

Also note: The punch line ended with an exclamation point: "Tip was the world's worst driver!" Punctuation plays a key role in good speechwriting. While the audience won't see a punctuation mark, the speaker certainly does. Plain and simple: Punctuation helps a speaker's delivery.

WHAT ABOUT DELIVERY?

I'm not funny. What I am is brave.

–LUCILLE BALL

A good delivery will greatly increase your chances of getting a good laugh.

You must be in complete control of the joke or anecdote. You must understand every word, every pause, every nuance. You must, above all, have a good sense of timing.

Want to see how important good delivery is? Practice this fifth-century line from Saint Augustine: "Give me chastity and continence, but not yet." The pause after "continence" makes the whole line.

Try another exercise: Read this one-liner from comedian George Carlin, emphasizing the word "everything" and pausing after "eighties." "I like Florida. Everything is in the eighties: the temperature, the ages, and the IQs." (Notice how the triad sets up the joke, so when "the IQs" comes, the audience is primed to laugh.)

Better yet: Visit YouTube to see Laura Bush's remarks at the 2005 White House Correspondents' Association dinner. She was terrific, and her timing was perfect. You can learn much about humor in speeches by watching her performance.

Listen to how she set up her humor:

> George always says he's delighted to come to these press dinners. Baloney. He's usually in bed by now.
>
> I'm not kidding.
>
> I said to him the other day, "George, if you really want to end tyranny in the world, you're going to have to stay up later."
>
> I'm married to the president of the United States, and here's our typical evening: Nine o'clock, Mr. Excitement here is sound asleep, and I'm watching *Desperate Housewives* [pause] with Lynne Cheney. Ladies and gentlemen, I am [strong emphasis] a desperate housewife."

A FINAL CAUTION

Don't set yourself up for failure by announcing, "Here's a funny story." Let the audience decide for themselves if it's funny or not. Be prepared in case the audience thinks it *isn't* funny. The only thing worse than the silence that follows a failed joke is the sound of the speaker laughing while the audience sits in embarrassed silence.

Don't laugh at your own jokes—ever.

NINE

SPECIAL-OCCASION SPEECHES

Act well your part: there all the honour lies.
—ALEXANDER POPE

Not all speeches deal with big issues. Many speeches are simply ceremonial. They honor a person's retirement, or present an award, or dedicate a new building. These speeches are different from the standard public speech. They're usually much shorter, and they often take a personal approach. This chapter will give some guidelines on:

- the invocation
- the commencement speech
- the award or tribute speech

It will also help you with some specialized speaking skills:

- How to introduce a speaker.
- How to give an impromptu speech.
- How to organize a panel presentation.
- How to present as a team.
- How to handle a question-and-answer session.

THE INVOCATION

The fewer words, the better the prayer.
                                        —MARTIN LUTHER

The scene: You're sitting on a dais at a banquet. The evening's event? To honor a local business executive with a humanitarian award.

Just before the banquet begins, the master of ceremonies learns that the clergyman who was supposed to offer the invocation can't attend. They need someone to fill in, and they turn to you. "Would you be kind enough to offer grace?"

Well, *would* you? Even more to the point, *could* you? Could you come up with an invocation that's appropriate for a mixed business gathering—a gathering that might include Christians, Jews, Muslims, and others?

Avoid prayers that represent a specific religious preference. Instead, say something that respects all people and the world we share—something that honors human dignity.

In a business setting, it's appropriate to:

- give thanks for blessings

- pray for peace

- ask for wisdom

- ask for the courage and strength to deal with your problems

Above all, keep it short—under a minute, if you can.

A word of caution about humorous invocations: *don't*. This is not the time to use a light touch. Avoid *anything* such as "Good food, good meat, good God, let's eat." (Yes, I'm told someone actually used that invocation at a civic organization.)

THE COMMENCEMENT SPEECH

Proclaim not all thou knowest.
                                    —BENJAMIN FRANKLIN

Everyone is in a good mood at a commencement. Students are glad to be finished with exams. Parents are glad to be finished with tuition bills. And instructors are glad to be finished with another academic year.

Don't let long-winded or pompous remarks put them in a bad mood.

Remember: Caps and gowns can be hot. Folding chairs can be uncomfortable. Crowded gymnasiums can be unbearably stuffy. Follow Franklin Delano Roosevelt's advice: "Be brief; be sincere; be seated."

In the process, of course, try to say something inspirational, thoughtful, encouraging, uplifting, or memorable.

Academy Award–winning actress Meryl Streep knew this when she returned to speak at her alma mater, Vassar College. She encouraged the graduates to strive for excellence, even though life might be difficult at times. "If you can live with the devil," Streep said, "then Vassar has not sunk its teeth into you." This proved to be a great line for a commencement speech—easy for the audience to remember, and irresistible for the press to quote.

It's safest to speak for between eight and twelve minutes. If you go on longer, the audience may get dangerously restless. After all, a graduating class doesn't have to worry anymore about reprisals from the school principal or the college president. They're free to yawn or talk or even boo. Don't make any remarks about the brevity (or verbosity) of your speech. I once heard a commencement speaker promise to be brief. He was, much to his embarrassment, applauded by a few rambunctious students.

Remember that June weather is notoriously fickle. If the

commencement is outdoors, be alert to the storm clouds and be prepared to shorten your address if the rains come.

Also, make sure your hat's on tight. More than one commencement speaker has been distracted by a hat flying off into the wind.

PRESENTING AN AWARD

Tis an old maxim in the schools,
That flattery's the food of fools;
Yet now and then your men of wit
Will condescend to take a bit.

—JONATHAN SWIFT

A person who retires after forty years of service, an employee who contributes a money-saving idea to the company, and a telephone installer who saves a customer's life—all of these people deserve some special recognition, and you may be asked to give a speech in honor of one of them. These five guidelines should help:

1. *Be generous with the praise.* If one of your employees risked his life to save a customer's life and he's now receiving a special award, you must come up with praise to match the occasion. Be generous.

2. *Be specific.* Whatever you say should be so specific that it couldn't possibly be said about anyone else. Never, *never* give an award speech that sounds canned. For example, if the person is retiring after forty years with the company, mention two or three specific projects he was involved in. Tell how his involvement made a difference.

3. *Be personal.* Make your tribute reveal a flesh-and-blood person. Show the honoree's personality and vulnerability. One good way to personalize your presentation: Ask the honoree's

friends and family for some special recollections. Include a few of these "real-life" stories when you make your presentation.

4. *Be sincere.* Suppose you must give an award to a person you've never met. Don't pretend to be a close friend or associate. Simply get some information about the person from a supervisor and share this information in a sincere, straightforward way. For example, "Karen's supervisor has told me how Karen saved a baby's life. I'm glad to meet Karen and to present her with this award for distinguished service. I'm proud to have her as one of our employees."

5. *Be inspirational.* The Reverend Peter Gomes said this in a memorial tribute to Martin Luther King Jr. at Harvard University: "We remember Martin Luther King Jr. not because of his success, but because of our failures; not because of the work he has done, but because of the work we must do."

INTRODUCING A SPEAKER

Your assignment is to introduce a speaker. That's simple. Just call the speaker and ask for a written introduction—not a résumé or a vita, but a completely written introduction that you can deliver.

WHAT A GOOD INTRODUCTION SHOULD INCLUDE

A good introduction should be brief—certainly no more than three minutes, and preferably just a minute or two. It will let the audience know:

- Why it is that *this speaker*
- from *this organization*

- is talking about *this topic*

- to *this audience*

- at *this time.*

A good introduction should present this information in a friendly, personal way. It should *not* sound like a résumé. It should *not* sound like a repetition of the biographical data already printed on the program.

If the speaker provides you with a stuffy introduction, rewrite it to sound friendlier. For example, delete a boring list of professional organizations and fill in with an anecdote that shows what kind of person the speaker is.

If the introduction provided is too modest, add some material that shows the speaker's unique qualifications. Quote the speaker, if possible, or quote someone else's remarks showing the speaker's special attributes.

Introduction dos

- Be sure to pronounce the speaker's name correctly. (Verify the pronunciation in advance.) Repeat the speaker's name several times during the introduction so the audience can catch it.

- At the end of the introduction, face the audience (*not* the speaker) and announce the speaker's name: "We couldn't have found a more qualified hospital administrator than . . . Peggy Smith."

- Then turn to the speaker and smile.

- In formal situations, applaud until the speaker reaches your side, shake hands, and return to your place.

- In informal situations, sit down as soon as the speaker rises and starts toward the lectern.

- Pay close attention to the speaker's opening. It may contain a reference to you, and you should be prepared to smile or nod in response.

- Plan these movements carefully. Make sure the speaker knows the last line of your introduction so he or she can use it as a cue.

Introduction don'ts

- Don't upstage the speaker by making your introduction *too* funny. (Let the speaker be the star.)

- Don't try to present a capsule summary of the speaker's speech. (You might misinterpret the speaker's focus, and that would put the speaker at a serious disadvantage.)

- Don't steal the speaker's material. (If the speaker told you a good anecdote over lunch last week, don't use it. The speaker might have planned to use it in the speech.)

- Don't rely on memory. (Write out your introduction in full.)

- Don't ad-lib. (Many a "spontaneous" comment has turned into an inane one—especially after a few drinks.)

- Don't draw attention to any negative conditions. (For example, don't say, "We're glad that Josephine has recovered from her heart attack and that she can be with us today." Comments like this do *not* put an audience in a relaxed mood.)

- Don't try to con the audience by saying things such as, "This is the funniest speaker you'll ever hear." (Let the audience make up their own minds.)

- Don't put pressure on the speaker by saying, "Now we'll see whether or not he's an excellent speaker, which I expect he is." (I once heard a CEO make such an introduction, and the speaker looked terrified.)

FIVE CLICHÉS THAT NEVER WORK
IN AN INTRODUCTION

These clichés do a disservice to you and to the poor speaker who must follow your introduction. Avoid:

1. "Ladies and gentlemen: here is a speaker who needs no introduction. . . ."
2. "Her reputation speaks for itself. . . ."
3. "Without further ado . . ."
4. "Ladies and gentlemen: heeeere's . . ."
5. "We are a lucky audience to get anyone willing to substitute at the last moment . . ."

I have heard all these introductions used by supposedly intelligent people. I wished I had not, and so did the rest of the audience.

THE IMPROMPTU SPEECH

Mark Twain once said, "It usually takes more than three weeks to prepare a good impromptu speech." Alas, he was right. If you're going to a meeting where someone *might* ask you to speak, gather your thoughts in advance.

Ask yourself, "What is likely to happen at this meeting? Who will be there? What will they probably say? Are there any controversial areas? Will people have questions for me? How should I respond?"

Make notes about the topics you think will come up. Practice some impromptus until you are comfortable and convincing. Be sure to practice *aloud*. Your thoughts can't count until they're spoken—and heard.

Perhaps the worst thing that can happen at a meeting is for

someone to ask you for an answer, opinion, or analysis, and the request catches you totally off guard. You've never given the subject a thought. You don't have any facts or figures. You're in deep trouble, right?

Not necessarily. If you have poise, your audience will forgive you almost anything. Keep your head high, your back straight, your shoulders relaxed, your eyes alert, your voice strong, your pitch moderate.

Above all, don't apologize. Never say anything like, "Oh, I'm so sorry. I feel so embarrassed. I didn't know you'd ask me to speak. I don't have any information with me."

No one expects you to give a keynote address under these circumstances. Just make a comment. If you can't come up with an intelligent response, keep your poise, maintain direct eye contact, and say, in an even voice, "I don't know. I will look into that and get back to you with the information."

HOW TO ORGANIZE AN IMPROMPTU SPEECH

- Decide what you want to talk about—*fast!*

- Commit yourself to that approach. Don't change subjects or reverse your opinion midstream.

- Feel free to pause for a few seconds to collect your thoughts. The audience will not think you're stupid; they'll admire you for being able to organize your ideas under difficult circumstances.

- Open with a generalization to stall for time, if necessary. "Deregulation is certainly an important issue right now" will buy you a few extra seconds to compose your response.

- Or, repeat the question to stall for extra time. "You're asking me about the changes that deregulation will bring to our industry." Repeating the question has an extra benefit: It makes sure the audience knows what you've been asked to speak about.

- Present just two or three points of evidence. Do not bore the audience with chronological details.

- Wrap up your impromptu speech with a firm conclusion—a punch line that people can focus on.

- Do not ramble. Once you've offered what sounds like a conclusion, just stop.

PANEL PRESENTATIONS

HOW TO MODERATE

- Seat the panelists three or four minutes in advance—just long enough to allow them to get their papers in order, not long enough for them to look awkward as they wait.

- Make sure they have glasses of water, with extra pitchers on the table.

- Remind them to turn off their cell phones.

- Use large name cards to identify the panelists (by first and last names).

- Start the presentation on time. Make sure a clock is in full view of your panelists.

- Introduce yourself right away. I once heard a moderator, an editor, ramble on for seventeen minutes before she gave her name. The members of the audience kept whispering to each other, "Who is she? Who is she?" I'm sure they were also wondering, "What's she doing up there?"

- Make sure the audience is comfortable. If people are standing at the back of the room, tell them there are seats available at the front, then pause and allow them to move forward. If you don't take care of these logistics at the beginning, you'll be bothered by rustling noises throughout the panel presentation.

- As you introduce the panelists, use their names two or three times. Unless you are introducing J. D. Salinger, do *not* use initials. Give everyone a first name.

- Tell the purpose of the panel presentation.

- Explain *how* the panel will work (number of minutes allowed for each panelist, time for rebuttals, questions and answers, etc).

- Give the panelists a "thirty-second signal" so they can wrap up their presentations. One effective technique is to simply show the panelist a 3" × 5" card that reads "30 seconds."

- If panelists run over time, interrupt them—nicely, of course—and give them fifteen seconds to finish.

- *Do not* let any panelist abuse your schedule. Say in a firm, even voice, "Thank you, Mrs. Smith, but your time is up."

- Close the presentation on schedule with a few words of thanks to the panelists and to the audience.

HOW TO BE A PANELIST

- Be prepared for the worst. Inexperienced moderators may not know the above guidelines. Try to make the best of the situation.

- If the moderator forgot name cards or didn't pronounce your name properly, start by saying, "Hello. I'm *(name)*."

- If the moderator didn't give you an adequate introduction, briefly give your credentials and explain why you're there. However, do not criticize the moderator's oversight.

- Give your presentation a good title. This accomplishes several things: First, it clarifies your specific role on the panel; second, it sets the tone of your message; and third, it presents a more professional speaking image. Anthony Santomero, as president of the Federal Reserve Bank of Philadelphia, used this straightforward title when he spoke at the National Association for Business Economics: "What Monetary Policy Can and Cannot Do."

- If you are the last speaker and the time has run out, know how to give a shortened presentation.

- If another panelist refuses to stop speaking and the moderator can't control the situation, you may be forced to assert yourself. Do so with confidence—perhaps even a modicum of joy. I've had to stop a few long-winded panelists in my career. I wasn't embarrassed to step in—not at all. In fact, I considered my efforts to stop their run-on presentations as public service!

SOME TIPS FOR TEAM PRESENTATIONS

For many organizations, team presentations have become a way of life. Certainly, a well-orchestrated team presentation can pack a real wallop—but it also poses serious pitfalls. Know what you're dealing with.

Here are some suggestions:

Prior to the presentation:
1. *Make one person responsible.* This team leader will need to manage the entire project, from initial brainstorming sessions to final dress rehearsals.

2. *Set the date for your dress rehearsal.* Do this up front—and make it firm. What's the best time to rehearse? One full day prior to the actual presentation. You want enough time for speakers to make *minor* changes to their material or slides—but not enough time to fall into the temptation of making *major* changes! (This is one of the biggest problems I've seen as a speech coach. Speakers get to the rehearsal and frantically decide to rewrite their whole presentation, leaving no time for practice.)

3. *Hire a presentation coach early in the process.* Good speech coaches are booked well in advance. Don't wait until the last minute to hire yours.

4. *Keep everyone informed.* Keep everyone in the loop for meeting schedules, content themes, visual concepts, production deadlines, handout requirements, and rehearsal schedules.

5. *Clarify each person's function in writing.* It isn't enough for Bob to know what he's supposed to do. Everyone else has to know what Bob should do as well. "Who's doing the PowerPoint?" is a question you never want to hear. Prevent confusion by writing clear, direct to-do lists, with no wiggle room.

6. *Capitalize on the unique strengths of your team.* Who has the most pleasing voice? Choose that person to welcome the audience. Who has the strongest storytelling skills? Tap that person to kick off your presentation with a riveting example. Who's the most persuasive person? Ask her to present controversial material. Who has the best technical skills? Have him handle any demonstrations. Who knows the audience best? Let him moderate the questions and answers.

7. *Work around weaknesses.* If Sue typically spends too much time explaining the charts, let someone else do that section of the presentation.

8. *Build continuity.* Make sure each speaker's message connects with the rest of the team. Use smooth transitions. Ruthlessly cut duplication. (Your team members should *reinforce* each other, not *repeat* each other. There's a difference.)

9. *Incorporate a series of deadlines.* Multiple deadlines keep everyone on track and assure a better final product. Dress rehearsals are *not* the time to learn that Sam based his presentation on faulty research.

10. *Plan the dress rehearsal carefully.* Pay attention to timing. Multiple pass-offs can be time-consuming, and technology demonstrations often take longer than anticipated.

At the presentation:

1. *Get every presenter settled at the same time.* If three team members arrive on stage at 9:15, but the fourth team member doesn't arrive until almost 9:30, well, that sends a signal to the audience—a bad signal.

2. *Give each member a good introduction.* You'll find detailed advice about "introductions" in my earlier book, *Can You Say a Few Words?* (St. Martin's Press, updated 2006).

3. *Listen to each other's presentations.* Active listening means: good eye contact, attentive body language, appropriate smiles, and occasional nods of agreement.

4. *Control the question-and-answer session carefully.* It's embarrassing when one presenter gets all the questions, while the rest of the team just sits there like well-dressed mannequins. Encourage participation. You want your Q&A to have a team spirit, and to flow as smoothly as the presentation itself.

QUESTION-AND-ANSWER SESSIONS

There aren't any embarrassing questions—just embarrassing answers.
            —AMBASSADOR CARL T. ROWAN JR.

A question-and-answer session can make or break your speech. Plan to make the Q&A work *for* you, not *against* you.

You should prepare for a Q&A as carefully as you prepare for a speech. Always develop a list of possible questions. Be realistic. If you're giving a speech on a controversial topic, you can expect to receive tough questions.

Consult with the people in your business who work close to the news—for example, the consumer advocate, the treasurer, the public relations staff. Have them review your list of possible questions. Ask them to add to it.

Don't be intimidated by the difficulty of these questions. Don't allow yourself to be placed in a defensive position. Instead, come up with answers that work to *your* advantage. Practice these answers—*aloud*. It doesn't do any good to plan an assertive response if you can't sound assertive when you give it.

Here are ten practical tips to help you with a question-and-answer session:

1. *Take questions from all parts of the audience.*
2. *Listen carefully to each question.* Don't smile or frown excessively as you listen—save your response until it's time for you to answer. Don't nod your head enthusiastically to show you understand the question. The audience may think you automatically agree with the questioner.
3. *Pay attention to your posture and body language.* Avoid any fidgeting motions that might reveal anxiety. Never, for example, click a pen while you are being asked a question.

4. *Treat every questioner as an equal.* Don't try to compliment someone by saying, "Good question." It implies the others were *not* good questions. Be especially careful not to brush off questions from your subordinates or to fawn over comments from your superiors.

5. *Repeat all positive questions.* This makes sure the audience has heard the question. It also buys you a few seconds of time to prepare your response.

6. *Paraphrase the negative questions.* This allows you to set the tone and to control the emphasis of your answer. *Don't* repeat any hostile language (e.g., "Why did we fire all the older workers who had been with the company for so many years?"). If you repeat it, you might be quoted as actually saying it.

7. *Look first at the person who asked the question.* Then establish good eye contact with the whole audience as you give the answer.

8. *Respond simply and directly.* If your response is too long, the audience may think you're trying to stall for time to avoid further questions.

9. *Don't extend your answers.* The more you say, the more chance you have to hang yourself. Remember what Calvin Coolidge said: "I have never been hurt by anything I didn't say."

10. *Don't limit yourself by saying, "This will be our last question."* If that question turns out to be a difficult one and you handle it poorly, you will end in a needlessly weak position. Instead, try saying, "We have a few minutes left. Can I take another question?" If you feel confident with the answer you give, then let this be the last question and wrap up the session. If you aren't satisfied to end the session at this point, you still have the option of accepting another question.

HOW TO HANDLE SPECIAL PROBLEMS IN A Q&A SESSION

- *If no one asks you a question.* Don't just stand there in silence. Ask yourself a question. Try, "Last week, when I spoke to the chamber of commerce, several people asked me about our plans to build a new plant. Perhaps I should spend a few minutes on that."

- *If someone asks about something you already discussed in the speech.* Answer anyway. Perhaps you didn't make your message clear enough. Try another approach. If you used an anecdote to explain something during your speech, use statistics or quotations to clarify the point during your Q&A. If the audience didn't understand your first technique, maybe they'll understand your second or third.

- *If someone repeats a question that's already been asked.* Don't answer it again. "I believe we've already answered that" will usually work.

- *If someone tries to turn a question into a long-winded speech.* Stop him or her politely but firmly. Interrupt the person's rambling and ask him or her to come to the point and give the question—"in the interest of saving time." The rest of the audience will appreciate this indication that you value their time. Gestures can help. When you interrupt the questioner, slowly raise your hand in front of you. This stop-sign signal will reinforce your words.

- *If someone asks a totally irrelevant question (perhaps about your personal life).* Just say, "Well, that's not what we're here to discuss." Period—end of discussion.

- *If someone asks a disorganized question.* Respond to only one part and ignore the rest. Naturally, pick the part of the question that will help you to reinforce your message.

- *If you don't know the answer.* Say so. Offer to get the information and send it to the person.

- *If you run out of time.* Say you're sorry you couldn't get to answer every question. Offer to make yourself available to people who want to pursue the subject further—perhaps during a coffee break or after the lunch.

HOW TO RESPOND TO HOSTILE QUESTIONS

You're the manager of consumer conservation at an electric utility, and you've just finished speaking to a community group about energy-saving ideas. Up pops a hand, and you hear this question: "How can you stand there and talk about conservation when thousands of old people in your service area are so poor? What do you want them to do? Pay high rates and eat cat food?"

How do you get out of this one? Very carefully.

Hostile questions are *not* impossible to answer. They just require special skills. Learn the techniques and practice them. Do it now, before you need to use these skills. Don't wait until you're put on the spot. It's too late then.

Start by giving yourself three basic rights:

- the right to be treated fairly

- the right to stay in control—of yourself and the situation

- the right to get your message across correctly

Remember:
You are the invited speaker. No one in the audience has the right to take your role or to obscure your message. Concentrate on getting your message across. In preparation for any Q&A, choose two or three important points that you can express as one-liners.

Memorize these lines. Use them as *focus statements* when the Q&A gets difficult.

Rephrase any hostile questions so you can get into a *focus statement*. For example:

> **Q:** "All of your fancy plans to put up these big apartment buildings will just tear up our streets and tear down our old homes. What do you want to do to our downtown area? Kill it?"
>
> **A:** "You're asking about our redevelopment plans." (rephrased question) *"Well, let me say that we plan to build a healthy downtown—where people can live and where businesses can do business."* (focus statement)

Don't be afraid of hostile questions. As Edmund Burke put it, "He who opposes me, and does not destroy me, strengthens me."

It's also imperative that you never insult anyone. "Well, I'd never insult anyone in a question-and-answer session. That would be mean—and dangerous." Is this what you're thinking to yourself?

You're right. It *would* be mean and dangerous to insult anyone during a Q&A. But unthinking speakers do it all the time. Let me share a few bad examples so you can learn from their lessons.

> **Person X:** "Why is the company authorizing so much stock? That's way too much!"
>
> **Speaker:** "Do you know the difference between issued and authorized stock? Issued stock is—"
>
> **Person X:** "Are you saying I don't know what I'm talking about?"

Don't accidentally insult a questioner's intelligence. Listen respectfully to the question, then try, "For the benefit of the whole audience, let me explain the difference between *issued* and *authorized* stock."

> **Person Y:** "Why didn't you do more testing on that drug before you sold it to the public?"
>
> **Speaker:** "If you'd been listening to my speech, you'd obviously know the answer to that question."

Don't embarrass questioners in public. They will never forget the humiliation, and they will hold it against you.

Warning:
"Obviously" can be an emotionally charged word. It often seems like a put-down. After all, if something was so obvious, why did the questioner miss it? Is he or she stupid?

A heckler dominated the Q&A session at an important meeting. The speaker grew increasingly frustrated, and finally threatened the heckler with, "I'm going to ask you to sit down in a few minutes."

Of course, the heckler just loved this attention, so he continued to interrupt the Q&A with long-winded questions. Each time, the speaker raised his voice and said, "I'm going to ask you to sit down soon."

Don't make idle threats. The heckler will love the extra attention, and the audience will think you are ineffectual. If you can't carry out a threat, don't make it.

> **Q:** "Why do you think your program is so much better than the one Fred Smith started, which we've been using for years?"
>
> **A:** "Well, there were lots of problems with the old program. For example . . ."

Don't criticize a predecessor's work. Even if Fred is no longer with the organization, he may have friends and relatives and loyal supporters who still are. They will resent you for knocking his work.

Instead, explain that you inherited a good structure, but that new information, subsequent events, increased funding, larger staff, or advanced technology allowed you to build on that foundation. For a strong emotional appeal, point out how Fred himself would have probably welcomed the chance to expand his original program: "At Fred's retirement dinner, he said the future seemed to be coming faster and faster—and that he wished he could be around to see all the changes in our industry."

Never give the impression that you've disregarded someone else's work, or the audience will think you are reckless and arrogant.

TIPS FOR TELEVISION INTERVIEWS

In the age of sound bites, the three-minute Gettysburg Address would have been two-and-a-half minutes too long. One of today's ambitious young correspondents would probably have summed it up this way: "The President himself admitted to this subdued Pennsylvania crowd what his men have been saying privately: That no one will long remember what he said here."

–RICHARD M. NIXON

Television brings us a wide range of morning interview shows, evening news programs, the late-night news, special crisis reports, weekly news analyses, profiles of executives, coverage of community events, local business updates, hard-hitting exposes, consumer advisories, and inside stories.

Of course, to keep all this news coverage running, television needs *people who will appear as guests*. Question: Will *you* be sitting in one of those interview chairs someday?

There are two basic ways to appear on TV:

1. Perhaps you'll be invited to promote something you're proud of. Some common situations:
   - An executive is eager to appear on TV so she can publicize a new fundraising effort.
   - A civic leader needs visibility so he can create support for a worthwhile community project.
   - A high-school principal welcomes the chance to talk about a unique educational experiment.

2. On the other hand, perhaps you'll be "summoned" to appear on a news program to defend, explain, or justify something that's potentially embarrassing to your organization. A sampling of crises:
   - food tampering
   - a car accident
   - a school fire of suspicious origin
   - teenage drinking
   - drug abuse on campus
   - criminal activity in the workplace
   - employee layoffs

No matter whether you're "invited" or "summoned" to appear on TV, either way, you've got to come across to the viewing audience with credibility, clarity, and competence. These TV interview tips should help:

BEFORE THE INTERVIEW

- *Set your objective.* Pick two or three key points you want to stress during the interview. Make them simple, powerful, and relevant.

- *Watch the program.* Observe the host's style. Is your interviewer generally friendly or antagonistic . . . pro-business or anti-business . . . concise or long-winded . . . well-prepared or prone to wing it?

- *Ask about the format.* Length of interview? Taped or live? Other guests? Number and duration of commercials? Policy on call-ins?

- *Provide accurate information.* Make sure the producer has an accurate description of your credentials. Clarify the proper pronunciation of your name.

- *Anticipate likely questions.* The best way to do this: Put yourself in the interviewer's shoes, then imagine the questions *you'd* ask in that situation.

- *Prepare effective answers.* Be brief, be specific, be helpful. Use terms the audience will understand. Be prepared with anecdotes the audience will enjoy. Use real-life situations the audience can relate to. Practice your answers aloud, and record them. Review the recordings: Cut any long parts, and spice up any dull parts.

- *Pay attention to your appearance.* How you look will be as important as what you say, so dress appropriately for the occasion. (Again, it pays to watch the program in advance. Ask yourself: "How will my outfit look against *this* particular set?") In general, be neat and be conservative. Whatever you do, don't let your clothes overpower your message.

DURING THE INTERVIEW

- *Arrive early.* Let's face it: TV studios can be downright over-whelming. The glaring lights, the high-tech cameras, the mul-tiple monitors, the hustle and bustle of assistant producers, the technicians' jargon—all are potentially intimidating.

  So, don't arrive at the last minute. Give yourself a chance to look around and get familiar with all the sights and sounds. Then, you can put these distractions aside and focus on the *important* thing: to give a good interview.

- *Concentrate.* Once the interview starts, you must give it your concentrated attention. Really *listen* to the interviewer's questions. Above all, listen for opportunities where you can reinforce your main points.

- *Be clear.* Don't hem and haw. Don't ramble. Don't filibuster. Open your answer with a simple statement ("That's right," "No, not really," "Absolutely," "That's a common misconception," "Yes, it's true."), then add the necessary details to support your case.

- *Be human.* Tell a personal story. Give a quick case history. Share a recent example. Use a lively quotation or a revealing anecdote. Tap into the emotions of the audience.

  All of these techniques will help you come across as a believable, trustworthy, and caring individual.

- *Be conversational.* Leave your jargon back at your office. Keep your boring statistics locked in your briefcase.

- *Be helpful.* Try to approach the topic from the audience's perspective. Give examples they can relate to. Offer solutions they can put into practice.

- *Be visual.* Television is a visual medium. If you've got terrific video clips, or relevant documents, or startling photographs, or interesting objects, use them to your advantage.

- *Use appropriate body language.* Beware of "grand movements." Sure, they might look great when you're standing at the lectern on a big stage, but when you appear on a small TV screen in someone's bedroom, those same movements can make you look downright silly. Another caution: Avoid repeatedly nodding "yes" as your interviewer asks questions. Just listen—then let your response reflect your opinion.

- *Take advantage of commercial breaks.* Use this time to collect your thoughts, to do a mental rundown, and to make sure you're getting in your basic points. Ask the host what's next—and even suggest a specific area you'd like to discuss (politely, of course).

- *Exude confidence.* After all, if *you* don't have faith in your own expertise, why should the audience?

- *Radiate charisma.* Sincerity and charm sell—and nowhere do they sell better than on TV. Remember that, and you can't go too wrong.

THE POWER OF A SHORT ANSWER

One time, Barbara Bush made the risky comment that New York City mayor Ed Koch was "full of it." Later, a reporter tried to grill her on this comment, wanting to know exactly what she meant, and no doubt hoping she'd stick her foot in her mouth. With classic Barbara Bush wit, she simply smiled and gave this answer: "Joy." Hard to do much better than that. I've admired the lady ever since.

HOW TO HANDLE TRICK QUESTIONS

Questions often fall into patterns. If you recognize the pattern, you can get around the question much better.

Be aware of these trick questions:

- *The "A" or "B" Question.* "Which is more important to your company—building a new production plant in our town or opening new offices out of state?" Don't pigeonhole yourself. Say, "They're both important," or "Those are just two of our concerns."

- *The Multiple Question.* "Will the university make a special effort to recruit minority students? And will the athletic program be more closely supervised? And will you build any more student housing?" Don't get confused by three or four questions at once. Answer one in detail, then accept questions from other people.

- *The Open Question.* "Tell me about your company." Here is where it pays to have pre-established *focus statements*. Use them to create the image you want.

- *The "Yes" or "No" Question.* "Will you have any layoffs next year—yes or no?" *Never* get forced into a yes or no. Make the statement in your own words.

- *The Hypothetical Question.* "What if the union doesn't accept this offer?" Avoid being pulled into "doomsday" situations. They're like bottomless pits. Cut off the discussion by saying, "We're confident we'll reach an agreement." Consider this exchange from a news conference with President Reagan:

  Q: "Mr. President, if there's no change in the situation, is there a time when you would want to bring the troops home?"

A: "Let me just say that—I got into trouble a little while ago from trying to answer a hypothetical question with a hypothetical answer. And various interpretations were placed on it." Reagan then avoided a hypothetical answer and gave a *focus statement* that summed up his position.

- *The Off-the-Record Question.* There is no such thing as an off-the-record question in a Q&A session. Answer all questions as though your answer will immediately appear in a major blog. It just might.

- *The Ranking Question.* "Would you name the top three concerns of today's teaching profession?" Again, don't pigeonhole yourself. As soon as you name the top three concerns, someone will ask, "What's the matter? Don't you care about *(blank)*?" Then you'll be stuck. Instead, try, "Among our most important concerns are . . ."

- *The Nonquestion Question.* "I don't think we need all this new equipment." How can you respond to such a statement? By converting it into a question. For example: "I'm hearing a question in your statement, and that question is, 'How can we benefit by using this equipment?'" Then, you can answer the question without having to rebut the original statement.

- *The False Premise Question.* "Now that you've dumped all that pollution into the river, how are you going to clean it up?" *Always* correct a false premise. Say in a firm voice, "That's not so. Let me set the record straight."

- *The Cross-Examination Question.* "Let's review the waste-disposal issue once again. What possible explanation can you give for this disgraceful situation?" If the questioner has sneaky motives, address them. Say, "That sounds like a trap.

What are you trying to get me to say?" *Remember:* You are not in a courtroom. You do not have to subject yourself to a cross-examination.

WHAT TO INCLUDE IN YOUR ANSWER

- *Cite your own professional experience.* "In my twenty-five years of work in this field, I have never seen anything like that."

- *Cite your own personal experience.* "Well, I just went out and bought a *(blank)*. I know the product's good."

- *Quote the experts.* "The top researchers in the country would disagree with you. At Columbia University, for example . . ."

- *Present facts.* "The fact of the matter is . . ."

- *Disassociate.* "That's like comparing apples and avocados. We can't be compared."

- *Establish a bond.* "Well, I can certainly understand how you feel. In fact, many people have felt the same way, but when they became more familiar with the program, they found out that . . ."

- *Simplify the numbers.* "Yes, $10,000 *does* seem like a lot of money to spend on training until you consider that this amounts to only 'x' dollars per person. The increased productivity will pay back our initial investment in just one year."

- *Recognize the importance of the question.* Some people don't want an answer. They just want to be heard. They want their day in court. If you recognize this need for attention, you will satisfy them. Play psychologist and say in your most soulful voice, "Sounds like that's an important issue to you." However, be careful not to sound patronizing.

- *Above all, include your focus statements.* Use those one-liners that will stick in the minds of the audience—and may be quoted by the press.

HOW TO USE A BRIDGING RESPONSE

Use a *bridging response* when you don't want to discuss the question. Listen to the question, then bridge to one of your focus statements by saying something like this:

- "Well, Paul, the really important issue we should be discussing is . . ."

- "Consumers would be better off if they asked about . . ."

- "That's not the critical issue here. The critical issue is . . ."

In each case, use the bridging response to get into a specific point you want to make. If possible, address the questioner by name. It produces a calming, persuasive effect.

USE HUMOR SPARINGLY—IF AT ALL

It's too easy for humor to backfire in a question-and-answer session. Why? Because it seems to be directed at a particular person. If you pick on someone the audience really likes, you're in trouble.

For example, "You'd better get to the point of your question because I'm only president of this organization for another eight months." Such a line might draw a laugh, but if you happen to say it to the wrong person, the audience may turn against you.

Of course, there's a flip side to this coin:

If a *questioner* says something funny, chuckle. Show you're human. Never try to top someone's line. Let that person have a brief, shining moment of glory. The audience will appreciate—and respond to—your good-naturedness.

HOW TO ANTICIPATE REAL-WORLD QUESTIONS

Before you speak to any audience, think of the questions you might receive. No presenter wants to be caught off-guard. This list should help you prepare.

1. What are the most likely questions for this audience/interviewer to ask?

2. What subject would I most like to address—and how could my organization benefit?

3. What subject would I prefer to avoid right now—and why?

4. Would any questions require extra research on my part?

5. What research sources would this audience find most impressive/persuasive?

6. What lines/phrases/statistics need to be included?

7. What words/numbers should be avoided?

8. Would any answer benefit from the use of props (charts, photos, demonstrations)?

9. What message do I want to sell—and how can I work that message into my Q&A?

10. What questions might arise from the day's news events?

11. What if nobody asks any questions?

PRE-PRESENTATION SELF ASSESSMENT

It's not enough to think about your audience. You also need to think about yourself: What do you, as a speaker, want to accomplish? Use these questions to sharpen your focus.

1. What is my professional goal in this presentation?

2. Do I have any personal goals to keep in mind? (i.e., Are there specific people in the audience I'd like to meet?)

3. What must I say to achieve my goals?
   What must I *avoid saying*?

4. How do I want the audience to *feel* after they have heard me?
   What do I want them to *do*?

5. What makes me most uncomfortable with this presentation? (Can any of this be changed/prevented?)

6. What part of the presentation do I deliver the best?
   Why is my delivery better in certain sections?

TEN

THE NITTY-GRITTY DETAILS

*I never dared step into the pulpit without every-
thing, including the Lord's Prayer and the announcements, fully written out in front of me.*
—FREDERICK BUECHNER

Why worry about giving a speech? You'll be much better off if you put your time and energy into planning the speech.

Think about the logistics of giving your presentation. Plan for the unexpected and the unwanted. Then prepare, prepare, prepare.

This chapter will show you how to:

- prepare *your speech* for delivery by typing the manuscript in an easy-to-read script format

- prepare *the room* by controlling the physical layout

- prepare *audiovisual materials* that work for you, not against you

HOW TO TYPE A SPEECH

Type your speech so that:

- it is easy for you to deliver

- it is easy for the media to read

- it is easy for a substitute speaker to deliver if you are unable to speak

Proper manuscript preparation takes some extra effort, but your efforts will pay off.

Here are twenty-two tips from the professionals:

1. Type the manuscript in a large-size font.

2. Use upper and lower case. NEVER TYPE IN ALL CAPS.

3. Use a ragged right margin. Never justify the right margin. (I review hundreds of speeches each year, and I am amazed by the number of justified right margins I see. Do not ignore this very basic rule.)

4. Identify the speech on the top left corner of the first page with:
   - your name and title
   - the title of the speech
   - the name of the audience
   - the city you're speaking in
   - the date of the speech

5. Double-space between lines. Triple-space between paragraphs.

6. Start typing the speech about three inches from the top of the first page. This gives you space to make last-minute additions to your opening.

7. Be sure to end each line with a complete word. *Never* hyphenate words at the ends of lines. Leave the line short rather than hyphenate.

8. Don't break statistics at the end of a line. For example: "At our company we spend five hundred dollars a week on maintenance." (If you break after "five," you might

accidentally say "five thousand dollars" and would then have to correct yourself.)

9. End each page with a complete paragraph. It's too dangerous to start a sentence on one page and finish it on another page. You can lose too much time while shifting pages.

10. Be sure to leave at least three to four inches of white space at the bottom *of each* page. If you try reading copy that runs all the way to the bottom of the page, your head will bend too far down and the audience won't be able to see your face. Plus, if you have to bend your face down to read lines at the very bottom of a page, your volume will decrease and the audience might miss what you're saying.

11. Leave wide margins at the left and right of the copy.

12. Number each page on the upper right.

13. Use hyphens when you must pronounce each letter individually. (For example, "M-B-A degree" or "F-A-A regulations" or "C-I-A operations".)

14. Spell out foreign words and names phonetically. For example, after "Mr. Chianese," write "Mr. Kee-uh-NAY-zee" in parentheses.

15. Don't use Roman numerals in the script. They're fine for written presentations, but not speeches. It would sound stilted to say, "Now, Roman numeral one . . ."

16. Underline (or boldface) words or phrases that require emphasis.

17. Use an ellipsis (three dots, . . .) to mark slight pauses. This is often useful at the end of a paragraph, to remind you to pause for a second before proceeding.

18. Mark longer pauses with two slash marks (//). These slash marks remind you to stop for a few seconds, either to give

the audience time to laugh or to give you time to change the direction of your speech. If you use slash marks, be sure to drop down a couple of lines before you start typing again.

//

Like this. Otherwise, you'll obscure the marks.

19. At the end of the speech, include both e-mail and postal addresses where people can write for more information.

20. Never staple the pages of your speech together. Simply fasten them with a paper clip, which can be easily removed when you're ready to speak.

21. Place the manuscript in a plain, dark folder—ready for your delivery.

22. Always prepare a spare copy and carry it separately. For example, if you're going to deliver an out-of-town speech, carry one copy in your briefcase and another in your suitcase. (By the way: I included this tip in the original 1984 edition of the book. A reader wrote to tell me this advice had spared her a disaster when her suitcase was lost.)

Caution:

None of these rules will help you much if you forget to bring the speech along—or, if you mistakenly grab another document on your way to the lectern. In England years ago, a vice-admiral stood up to speak to the Royal Navy Old Comrades Association. After taking a careful second look at his notes, he was forced to end even before he began.

His confession to the puzzled audience? "By mistake, I brought a shopping list my wife gave me."

Tip:
When people in the audience ask you to send copies of your speech, have them put their requests on the back of their business cards. You'll have completely accurate e-mail information—with no possibility of error due to handwriting issues.

HOW TO PREPARE THE ROOM

It's amazing how many good speeches have been ruined by a nonfunctioning microphone or miserable lighting or a poor ventilating system.

You may have prepared a wise and witty speech, but if the audience can't hear you or see you, who cares?

And if the audience is suffering from an air-conditioning system that doesn't work, you might as well wrap it up early and head home.

Check out the room before you speak. If you can't go in person, view it online. Contact the person who invited you to speak to ask these basic questions:

- *Does the room have unwanted mirrors?* When I attended a conference of the American Society of Journalists and Authors in New York City, I watched award-winning writers make their acceptance speeches in a most unnerving setting. The hotel (a prestigious one) had placed the lectern directly in front of a massive mirror, so the audience got a rear-end view of each presenter.

    No speaker wants to appear in such a vulnerable and unflattering position—with nervous mannerisms on full view for all to see (tapping toes, crossing and uncrossing feet, fiddling at attire). Plus, huge mirrors destroy a speaker's privacy, making it hard to place notes or hide a stopwatch without the audience seeing.

Insist that a hotel either cover the offending mirror or move the lectern.

- *Does the room have windows?* Even more important, do the windows have heavy drapes? You'll need to close them if you show slides.

  You'll also need to close the drapes if you're speaking in a motel conference room that looks onto a swimming pool. There's *no way* you can compete with outdoor entertainment, so shut those drapes before the audience arrives and save yourself a lot of frustration during the speech.

- *Is there a lectern?* Does it have a light? Is it plugged in and ready to go? Is a spare bulb handy?

  Does the lectern have a shelf underneath where you can keep a glass of water, a handkerchief, a few cough drops?

  Can the lectern be adjusted to the proper height? If you're short, is there a sturdy, solid box to stand on? Move everything into place *before* you arrive at the lectern to speak. It's your right to feel as comfortable as possible.

- *Can you be heard without a microphone?* If so, don't use one.

  Too many speakers have the misconception that a microphone will improve their voice. It won't. It will just make their voice *louder.* So, if you normally mumble, a microphone will give you a louder mumbling voice. If you often interject "uh" or "like" or "mmm" into your speeches, a microphone will give you louder interjections.

- *Is the public address system good?* Test it and ask an assistant to listen to you. Must you stoop or lean to reach the microphone? It should be pointed at your chin.

  Can you be heard in all corners of the room? Is the volume correct? Do you get feedback? Where do you turn the microphone on and off?

- *How about the lighting?* Do a test run with the houselights. Do they create a glare when you look at the audience? In general, the light level on you should be about the same as the light level on the audience.

  Does a crystal chandelier hanging over your head create a glare for the audience? Remove the bulbs. Will the spotlight appear where it should? Adjust it.

- *What about the seating?* After they've taken off their coats and seated themselves and gotten comfortable, people hate to be asked to move. Perhaps it reminds them of school days. So, if you want to rearrange the seating, be sure to do it *before* the audience arrives.

  Will people be seated at round dining tables, with some of their backs to you? If so, allow time for them to shuffle their seats before you start to speak.

  It's difficult to maintain eye contact when listeners are scattered around a large room.

  If you expect a small crowd, try to remove some of the chairs before the audience arrives. Do anything you can to avoid "gaps" in the audience where energy can dissipate.

  If you'll speak in a large auditorium, have the rear seats roped off. This forces the audience to sit closer to you. This roped-off area is also great for latecomers. They can slip in without disturbing the rest of the audience.

  If only a few people show up, move your lectern from the stage to floor level to create more intimacy. Some years ago I was asked to give a presentation in Kansas City. The audience was smaller than the conference planners had estimated, so I simply took my lectern off the high stage and moved it to audience level. It made a huge difference.

  Never allow space to create a distance between you and your audience. The closer you are to your listeners, and the closer your listeners are to each other, the more successful you will be.

- *Is there good ventilation?* Can the air-conditioning system handle large crowds? Can the heat be regulated?

   Hotels are notoriously stuffy. One time I had to give a speech at a big hotel in New York City, and when I arrived two hours early, I found the room temperature about eighty degrees. I immediately got a hotel person to push that thermostat way back. By the time the audience arrived, the room was comfortable.

Rule:
Always arrive well ahead of your audience, so you can make these necessary changes more easily.

- *How many doors lead into the room?* Can you lock the doors at the front of the room to prevent intruders from upstaging you? Can you have assistants posted at the rear doors to ensure quiet entrances from latecomers and quiet exits from people who must leave before you finish?

- *Is music being piped into the room?* If so, turn it off immediately. Do not rely on hotel staff to do so when it's your time to speak.

- *Is the room soundproof?* This becomes a critical issue when you speak in a hotel room. Who knows what will be happening in the room next to yours: a raucous bachelor party, or an enthusiastic sales rally. What audience would concentrate on, say, cogeneration if they could listen to the excitement happening next door?

   Perhaps you think these things don't happen. Perhaps you think I'm making them up. Perhaps you think you don't have to worry about such minutiae. Well, this stuff does happen—all the time. I attend dozens of presentations each year, and I see the horror stories firsthand.

Once I could hardly concentrate because so much raucous noise was coming from an adjacent room. (Apparently, a sales rally was in full swing.) Finally, I wrote a note and asked someone in my audience to take it to the adjacent room, asking the person in charge to kindly keep the cheering and stomping at a reasonable level. The situation improved immediately—but only because I took steps to stop it. FYI: A written note is the best way to handle this. It avoids a one-on-one interaction that could be awkward. Quietly hand the note, then depart without saying anything else.

So, be assertive. Don't let anything get in the way of your success. Why should you spend weeks planning a great presentation, only to let something hinder your audience's listening comfort—or hinder your delivery?

Don't take any chances. If possible, make an unannounced visit to the hotel to check things out for yourself. Hotel managers routinely say their conference rooms are "nice and quiet." I say, follow the advice of President Reagan: Trust, but verify.

If you find that sound carries through the walls, speak to the manager. Ask to have the adjacent rooms empty during your speech. Naturally, if the hotel is booked solid, they won't be able to accommodate your request, but it doesn't hurt to ask.

- *Where can you find help?* Get the name and number of a maintenance person you can call or text for immediate attention. Someone who can step right in and replace a fuse or a lightbulb, or adjust the air conditioner. Keep this person's name and number handy at all times. Be very nice to this person.

Emerson was right. *Shallow* men believe in luck.

WHAT CAN YOU CONTROL IN A SPEECH OR PRESENTATION?

As the invited speaker, you have much more control than you might realize. Make full use of your authority!

Take a few minutes right now to think about the many aspects of your presentations and then decide whether you have NO control . . . SOME control . . . or TOTAL control. (Most speakers find they have TOTAL control over many of the factors listed below.)

	No Control	Some Control	Total Control
1) Your preparation	☐	☐	☐
2) Your notes	☐	☐	☐
3) Your attitude	☐	☐	☐
4) Your appearance	☐	☐	☐
5) Your prompt arrival	☐	☐	☐
6) Your own comfort*	☐	☐	☐
7) Your props	☐	☐	☐
8) Your words	☐	☐	☐
9) Your voice/tone	☐	☐	☐
10) Your body language	☐	☐	☐
11) Your eye contact	☐	☐	☐
12) When it's scheduled	☐	☐	☐
13) Where it's scheduled	☐	☐	☐
14) Other speakers	☐	☐	☐
15) Length of speech	☐	☐	☐
16) Q&A	☐	☐	☐

*access to cough drops, tissues, water, coffee/tea, snacks, headache medicine, etc

HOW TO USE AUDIOVISUAL AIDS

More speeches are ruined by audiovisual aids than are improved by them. I caution all speakers to be especially careful here. Don't ruin a first-rate speech with audiovisual materials that are second-rate, or even unnecessary.

A-V aids are unnecessary if they:

- contribute no new information to your speech

- fail to help the audience understand or appreciate your message

- actually *detract* from your role as speaker

Unfortunately, most speakers use audiovisual aids as a crutch. An all-too-common example: The speaker says, "I want to tell you about our new hiring program," and then flashes a slide that reads "New Hiring Program." Does this slide contribute any new information? No. Does this slide really help the audience to understand the speaker's message? No. Does this slide detract from the speaker's presence? Unfortunately, yes.

Speeches are designed primarily for the ear, but visuals are designed for the eye. If you are trying to talk while people are looking at words on a screen rather than at you, your words won't be as powerful. Your eye contact with the audience won't be as strong. In short, your message won't be as effective.

Need convincing? Try holding an important conversation on the telephone while looking at a television show. How much information will you miss?

If you really need to use audiovisual aids—to simplify complex information or to create an emotional appeal—use them wisely.

One effective technique is to use an audiovisual insert. Prepare a short slide show or a videotape and insert this into your speech as a self-contained unit. The audience can concentrate on the audiovisual segment and then return concentration to the remainder of your speech.

POWERPOINT

People are not listening to us, because they are spending so much time trying to understand these incredibly complex slides.
—SECRETARY OF THE ARMY LOUIS CALDERA

PowerPoint 1.0 went on sale in 1987—and it's safe to say, presentations haven't been the same since. Innumerable PowerPoint presentations are made every day.

Every sector of life uses PowerPoint: city zoning hearings, school board meetings, military briefings, corporate presentations, college and university presentations, sixth-grade book reports, even church announcements. Folks of all ilk use PowerPoint to communicate without even thinking about it. And therein lies the problem.

What started out as useful presentation software has run amok. Too many people give PowerPoint presentations because . . . well, "because everyone else is giving them." And that's a pitiful excuse.

PowerPoint use has degenerated into abuse—with so many spinning pie charts and exploding images, the main message gets lost in a kaleidoscope of bells and whistles. Is it any wonder we see a backlash? Savvy executives now know they can distinguish themselves from other presenters by appearing at a conference *as the only speaker without* the ubiquitous PowerPoint.

In 2000, General Hugh Shelton, chairman of the Joint Chiefs of Staff, made news when he told U.S. military bases around the world to stop the escalating use of presentation software. (Apparently, all those e-mailed military briefings were taking up too much classified bandwidth.) General Shelton had the guts to tackle communication's most sacred cow. I've admired the man ever since.

The truth is: The *power* is really in the *point*. No gradient color backgrounds can compensate for poor content, and no sound effects can hide poor delivery. I counsel my clients to *ditch the PowerPoint glitz*—urging them, instead, to craft a powerful message and to polish an appealing delivery.

Too many speakers lose time messing around with Power-Point production—and not enough time honing their message, or improving their delivery skills.

This overuse of presentation software has become more than a communication problem: It's a productivity problem, as well. Previously, senior executives would delegate slide production, either asking their assistants to do the job or hiring freelance artists, but no more.

Today, highly paid executives waste endless hours trying to produce their own PowerPoint, only to end up with boring templates and amateurish visuals. That's not smart communication—and it's not smart business, either.

I'm reminded of that old saw, "The person who serves as his own attorney has a fool for a client." The same could be said about presenters. *The executive who serves as his own graphic designer has a fool for a client.*

If you're going to use any presentation software, use it for a reason—and use it well.

Designing a PowerPoint presentation

Everyone thinks they can design their own A-V. They can't. I know, because I've had to sit through countless PowerPoint presentations that violated the most basic design principles.

Justified right margins, drop shadows, needless fly-ins, endless spirals, pointless checkerboards, angled typography, reverse type, miniscule type size, internal capitalization, too much copy, too little white space—these are the hallmarks of ill-designed Power-Point. They make a presentation look hokey. They make a presenter look amateurish.

If you lack talent in graphic design (and most of us do), hire a talented pro to design your slides. You'll save a lot of time, and wind up with a much better product.

Yes, skilled design services cost money, but probably not as much as you think. You might even find a talented high school student or college art major willing to do the work as an intern, happy for the experience, the portfolio piece, and a good reference.

Writing a PowerPoint presentation

What's the single most important thing you can do to write better presentations? *Use slide headlines that sell your message.* For example:

- Ditch those all-too-common one-word titles, like "Efficiency." Instead, write a benefit-oriented headline that grabs your audience: "Improve Efficiency in Three Steps."

- Don't settle for a bland title like "Quarterly Sales." Instead, make your headline tell the success story: "Sales Soar in Third Quarter."

- Avoid merely listing a topic like "Environmental Costs." Instead, intrigue your audience with "Five Green Costs Nobody Likes to Talk About."

Delivering a PowerPoint presentation

What's the single most important thing you can do to improve your delivery when using slides? *Maintain strong eye contact.* Don't turn away from the audience to refer to the screen.

Pointing to your charts with shaky pens, quivery Laser pointers, and waggling fingers will not enhance your professionalism.

It will merely give the audience a good view of your back. Trust me on this: They did not come to see your back.

Instead, direct your audience to focus on key elements by using strong visual elements. Attract their eyes with a bold arrow, carefully boxed text, or maybe some underlining. You'll increase their comprehension—and maintain your stature as a presenter.

Here are some additional tips:

- Set written copy flush left, with a ragged right margin.

- Keep type uniform.

- Use upper- and lowercase letters.

- Limit capitalization. IF YOU INSIST ON TYPING YOUR SLIDES IN ALL CAPS, AS YOU SEE HERE, YOU WILL FORCE THE AUDIENCE TO READ SLOWER—AND YOU WILL ALSO REDUCE THEIR ABILITY TO COMPREHEND YOUR MESSAGE. Don't make this mistake. Limit the ALL CAPS style to headlines and occasional short phrases. Your audience will be much more comfortable when they see natural capitalization on your slides.

- Use normal spacing between words and caps. One space (not two) after a period.

- Keep headings uniform. Use smaller sizes on subheads to indicate relative importance.

- Use only a few lines of type on any slide.

- Use color on charts and graphs to add interest and to boost comprehension.

- Double-check everything to make sure it is in proper order.

- Everything on a slide must be visible to the people in the last row. Take a look at your visuals from the back of the room.

- Tape down cords so no one will trip.

- Leave each slide on the screen long enough for you to make your point, then move on to the next one. The audience's interest will flag if a slide is left on too long.

VIDEO CLIPS

- Only use video to *reinforce* your message. Remember your eighth-grade history teacher who played movies when she hadn't bothered to plan a real lesson? Don't make that mistake. Avoid entertainment for entertainment's sake. Your video clips should *supplement* a well-planned presentation, not replace it.

- Get in, get out—maybe a minute here, or a minute there. That's why they're called video "clips." If they run too long, they're called video "distractions." Know the difference.

- Use a consistent theme and style. Multiple video clips need to share a similar look, just like the rest of your presentation shares a similar look. Don't let your audience get lost in a mish-mash of clip styles.

- Pay attention to your technology. Check and adjust all equipment in advance. Have enough monitors available. The audience should not have to strain to see your video.

- Don't be afraid to use emotional appeal. Video is uniquely suited to offering slice-of-life material. For example, if you're giving a speech on the need to donate blood, try a short video showing the people who benefit from blood donations. Get close-ups of faces, of children holding their parents' hands, and of doctors comforting patients. Don't use "perfect" people. Use "real" people who look like your audience.

SOUND EFFECTS

In his role as mayor of New York City, Michael Bloomberg rang the bell at the New York Stock Exchange—and made it more than a ceremonial gesture with these words: "Since I'm probably the only mayor who was at one point in their life a member of the New York Stock Exchange, it was particularly fun to stand up there. There is nothing that is as much a symbol of New York as the New York Stock Exchange."

The Bucks County (Pennsylvania) chapter of Mothers Against Drunk Driving holds an annual ceremony to remember the thousands who are killed and injured each year in alcohol-related crashes. Throughout the service, a bell rings every thirty seconds—representing the losses suffered throughout the United States because of drunk drivers.

When Deborah Cohn, commissioner for Trademarks for the U.S. Patent and Trademark Office, spoke at a professional conference in Mumbai in 2013, she used terrific photographs to show trademarked products ranging from shoes to candy bars. She also played sound clips, so the audience could hear audio trademarks. Look for audio opportunities when you speak. Audiences often find sound effects to be the most memorable part of a presentation.

OBJECTS

Want to show off an interesting object, or hold up an unusual item, or share a powerful photo? Fine—just make sure everyone can see what you've got.

1. Lift it up in the air. High up, so everyone can see it.

2. Hold it steady for a few moments.

3. Then, move it slowly so everyone in the room has time to see it. (Be quiet while you're moving the object. Let people look

at it in silence. Otherwise, they won't be paying full attention to your words. Even worse, once the object is out of their view, they'll feel they're missing something if they continue to hear you explaining the item.)

CREATIVE PROPS

In a State of the Union address, President Ronald Reagan once held up forty-three pounds of federal budget documents for everyone to eyeball, then dropped them to the floor with a dramatic thud, promising he'd never approve any such budget.

When Mark Gearan was named communications director in the Clinton White House, he brought along his wife and fourteen-month-old daughter to the announcement. While the cameras clicked happily away, Gearan looked at his baby and quipped, "Any prop I can get." Of course, your props don't have to be quite so extreme.

EMERGENCY A-V KIT

If you plan to give a computer presentation, be realistic. Ask yourself, "What if I couldn't get an Internet connection right away? What if I suddenly got nervous and couldn't make my laptop work?"

Prepare carefully, but realize: Even with careful preparation, things can go wrong when you use technology. As a general rule, the more sophisticated the A-V, the more complex the problems. In reality, a multimedia presentation poses a whole lot more risks than a flip chart.

Carry an emergency kit to all presentations. Include:

- a second hard drive

- extension cords

- spare lightbulbs

- three-pronged adapters

- a multiple-outlet box

- lots of duct tape (you don't want anyone tripping over loose cords)

- scissors

- screwdriver

- pliers

- a small flashlight

After all, a speech that cost thousands to prepare can be ruined by the failure of a $1.19 lightbulb.

Prevent failure. Prepare carefully.

And, just as an extra precaution, pack some headache medicine in that emergency kit. Tech glitches can be stressful, and you don't want to be running around looking for headache medicine before you go on stage. (Honestly. Speakers tell me stories like this.)

COPYRIGHT ISSUES

If you think you'd like to:

- play the CD of an inspirational song during your award ceremony

- include some clever political cartoons in your next slide presentation

- show excerpts of a popular movie at a company employee meeting

- photocopy magazine articles to use as handouts

- reproduce artwork as illustrations for your presentation

- combine articles to use as a "course-pack" for your next training session

- photocopy parts of a book that your audience might find useful

If you think these are great ideas, think again.

U.S. copyright law protects the creator of the work. You cannot use that work (in any way) without the creator's permission—period. It is the creator's property, and the creator has the right to first, control its use, and second, charge for its use.

If you find yourself thinking:

- "It's just a small audience, so copyright doesn't matter."

- "We're a nonprofit organization. We don't have to pay any reprint fees, right?"

- "Hey, who will ever find out if I show an excerpt of this movie at my meeting?"

- "We've always photocopied articles to give as handouts at PTA."

If you're thinking anything like this—think again.

Copyright applies from the moment of creation, and you cannot use that work without permission—no ifs, ands, or buts. So, get permission. Make sure everything is clear regarding intellectual property and copyright.

Do you own the footage yourself? Then get a signed release from anyone who is captured on your video.

Any questions about copyright? Ask an attorney.

WHEN TO USE A-V

Ask yourself these questions before you plan to use PowerPoint (or any other audio-visual aids) in your presentation.

	YES	NO
1. Does it save time for the audience?	☐	☐
2. Will it make my presentation more interesting?	☐	☐
3. Is it necessary to communicate my points?	☐	☐
4. Is it worth my time to prepare?	☐	☐
5. Is it worth the money (hotel AV fees, etc)?	☐	☐
6. Is it worth the additional rehearsal time I'll need?	☐	☐
7. Can the entire audience see it clearly?	☐	☐
8. Is the type big enough to read?	☐	☐
9. Are the colors appropriate?	☐	☐
10. Does the design reinforce my message?	☐	☐
11. Is it accurate?	☐	☐
12. Have I proofed it carefully? Very carefully?	☐	☐
13. Would I be embarrassed if any of it got quoted in the media?	☐	☐
14. Can I operate it with confidence?	☐	☐
15. Do I have a backup plan in case of a tech glitch?	☐	☐
16. Can I maintain eye contact with my audience while using it?	☐	☐
17. Can I gesture to the screen without turning my back to the audience?	☐	☐

HOW TO PREPARE YOURSELF

When you give a speech, you want to look and sound your best. Don't leave these things to chance.

HOW TO LOOK YOUR BEST

Sometimes, the smallest clothing choice will make the biggest difference. When he hosted the historic meeting of Yasser Arafat and Yitzak Rabin on the South Lawn of the White House in 1993, President Clinton realized there were many things he couldn't control about that day—but one thing he could control was his tie. Clinton symbolically chose a tie with little trumpets on it—to trumpet the glory of Mr. Arafat and Mr. Rabin shaking hands at the accord.

Of course, not all speaking engagements are so monumental. Here are some general guidelines:

- *Don't wear brand-new clothes* to give a speech. New clothes haven't had a chance to "fit" your body. They often feel stiff and uncomfortable, and what could be worse than having a button pop off or a seam rip open when you gesture in the middle of your speech? Wear "old favorites" instead—clothes that fit well and move the way *you* move.

- *Dress conservatively* for most business functions. If in doubt about the suitability of a piece of clothing, don't wear it. Your appearance should not overshadow your message.

- *Never take clothing directly from storage to an event without inspecting it.* I made that mistake once, only to discover that moths had turned my favorite Italian wool knit into a buffet—and I appeared in public with holes.

For men:

- A dark suit—clean and well-pressed, of course (Navy blue or "banker's" blue is generally a color that conveys authority and elicits trust.)

- A long-sleeved shirt (White or blue look best under bright lights.)

- A conservative tie with a touch of red for power (an old politician's trick)

- Long, dark socks (The audience shouldn't see a patch of hairy leg when you sit down and cross your legs.)

- Well-shined shoes

- No pens sticking out of your shirt pocket, please

- No coins or keys bulging in your pants pockets

For women:

- A suit, dress, or pants (static-free and noncling, of course)

- No low necklines

- Be careful with your hemline if you will be seated on stage when you speak. Be especially careful with your hemline if you have to sit on bar stools while you speak. (This is a trend I've noticed over the past couple of years. More and more events are having the panels sit on bar stools on stage. The stated reason? "To create a more natural feel." The problem? Sitting on a bar stool is awkward and tiring—and, if you're wearing ill-fitting clothes, it's just plain embarrassing.)

I do a great deal of media training. One client hired me after she had a disastrous experience on a TV show. Apparently, in an effort to create a "natural" atmosphere, the show's producer decided to use bean-bag-type chairs. When the executive sat down, she felt like a little girl disappearing into that big soft marshmallow of a chair. She hated it. And when I saw the clips, I could see why she hated the experience. How could she possibly project credibility when forced to sit in what amounted to a play chair? She spent much of the interview trying (in vain) to get her skirt to cover her knees.

- Moderate heels—no spiked heels that will clomp as you cross a wooden floor

- No rattling jewelry

- Arrange to leave your purse/briefcase with someone in the audience. (Do not carry it to the podium. But do not let it sit unattended! Theft by professionals is an issue at any large venue.)

One final thought about attire: What you wear can mean as much as what you say. I'm thinking of Justin Welby, who was installed as the new Archbishop of Canterbury in 2013. He spoke on themes of simplicity and modesty. How fitting, then, that he gave his BBC interview wearing a $15 used suit—bought from Oxfam, the British charity, which "works to create a just world without poverty."

HOW TO SOUND YOUR BEST

- Treat your voice well. No cheering for the local football team the day before.

- Ask your doctor about using a humidifier the night before. If you're staying in a hotel room, fill the bathtub with water before going to sleep. Moisture in the air will help prevent a dry-throat feeling.

- Hot tea with honey and lemon is great for the voice. Use herbal tea for an extra calming effect. Chamomile tea can be particularly relaxing.

- Avoid carbonated beverages prior to speaking. And surely, I shouldn't have to tell you: No alcohol.

AMERICAN PRONUNCIATION OF CAPITAL LETTER ABBREVIATIONS

Here's a list of common abbreviations. In this structure, American vocal stress always goes on the *last* letter (or the *last* character). Read this list aloud to get a great vocal warm-up before your presentation. (Just like athletes need to warm up before a big game, speakers should do a vocal warm up before a big speech.)

US

USA

CDC

CEO

VP

IRS

UK

UN

NIH

FDIC

UPS

FED EX

OK

AAA (TRIPLE *A*)

E71 (E-SEVENTY-*ONE*)

9-11 (NINE-*ELEVEN*)

A+ (A-*PLUS*)

ELEVEN

DELIVERY

Sincerity is everything. If you can fake that, you've got it made.

—GEORGE BURNS, COMEDIAN

Practice makes perfect, the saying goes. Well, practice may not make you a perfect speaker, but it will certainly make you a better speaker. With the right coaching, you may even become a great speaker.

This chapter will coach you on:

- rehearsals

- executive presence

- voice control

- eye contact

- body language

It will also show you how to deal with two special concerns: nervousness and hecklers.

PRACTICING YOUR DELIVERY

Practice your *delivery*, not just your speech. It's not enough to know the *content* of your speech. You must also be comfortable with the gestures and pauses and emphases that will help get your message across to the audience.

To do this, practice the speech in six stages. First, familiarize yourself with the script itself. Then familiarize yourself with the delivery techniques you'll need.

1. *Begin by reading the speech aloud to yourself.* Record it. How long does it take? Where do you need to pause to avoid running out of breath in mid-sentence? Should you rewrite any sentences so they're easier to deliver? Do you need to vary your pace? How does your voice sound? Does it fade at the end of sentences?

   If you generally have trouble projecting your voice, try putting the recorder across the room while you practice. This trick *should force* you to speak louder.

2. *Deliver the speech standing in front of a mirror.* By now, you should be familiar enough with the material to look up from the manuscript fairly often. Concentrate on emphasizing the right parts. See how your face becomes more animated at certain points in the speech.

   Caution: Be sure to rehearse the entire speech each time you practice. Otherwise, you'll have a well-prepared beginning but a weak ending. Deny yourself the luxury of "backtracking." If you make a mistake during rehearsal—trip on a line or leave something out—don't go back and start again. Be realistic. How would you recover from a mistake in front of an audience? That's how you should recover from it during your rehearsal.

3. *Deliver the speech to a friend.* Try to simulate a realistic environment. Arrange multiple chairs to create the feel of an audience. Stand up. Use a lectern. (Don't have a lectern? Use a music stand. They're adjustable, lightweight, and inex-

pensive. In fact, many speakers decide to buy a portable music stand because they can adjust it exactly to their liking. When they go onsite, they get the familiar comfort of using their own stand, rather than being stuck with a bulky wooden lectern—which can be hard to move and impossible to adjust.)

If you need to put on glasses to see the script, now's the time to practice doing that unobtrusively. Practice moving the pages quietly to the side. Don't "flip" them over. Look at your listener.

By this point, you should have memorized the first 30–60 seconds of your speech and the last 30–60 seconds, moments when eye contact is most critical. Do *not* try to memorize the whole speech, or your delivery will sound stilted. Instead of memorizing, aim for internalizing. Focus on the ideas, not the individual words. Look up a lot to make sure you're getting those ideas across. It's this *eye contact* with an audience that animates a speaker.

Allow yourself to smile when it feels natural. Gesture with your hand to make a point. Let your face talk, too.

4. *Practice again before a small group.* Try to make good eye contact with each person. Play with your voice a little bit to keep your listeners' attention. Notice where it helps to speak faster, slower, louder, softer. Each time you rehearse, you will find yourself memorizing—internalizing—a bit more.

5. *Give it your best shot.* Consider this advice from Lord Chesterfield: "Aim at perfection in everything, though in most things it is unattainable. However, they who aim at it and persevere, will come much nearer to it than those whose laziness and despondency make them give it up as unattainable."

6. *If possible, practice on-site.* You'll feel more confident in a room that seems familiar. If you can't practice on-site, be

sure to arrive extra early so you can get comfortable with
the layout of the room before you begin your speech.

PRESENCE

A speech doesn't start when you begin to speak. It starts the moment you enter the room.

An audience will start to form an opinion of you as soon as
they see you. First impressions count. Make yours good.

Carry yourself with presence from the moment you arrive.
Be well-groomed. Don't carry loose papers. Walk in a confident,
businesslike manner. Be polite. Smile. Kindly hold the door for
someone. (This will get you thinking about other people instead
of yourself—the best cure for pre-speech jitters.)

Listen carefully to other speakers and respond appropriately.
Pay particular attention to the person who introduces you. All
eyes will be on you as you walk to the podium, so don't choose
that highly visible moment to button your jacket or wipe your
eyeglasses or sort your papers. Take care of those details *before*
you leave your chair.

Don't bother to hide the fact that you'll use a written text. Just
carry the speech at your side—not in front of your chest, where it
looks like a protective shield. If you plan to shake hands with the
person who introduced you, carry the speech in your left hand so
you don't have to make a last-minute switch.

Never place your speech on the lectern in advance. The speaker
ahead of you might carry it away accidentally, and then you'd be
stuck.

When you get to the lectern, take care of "The Big Seven"—
preparations you can't afford to skip:

1. Open your folder and remove the paper clip from your
   speech. Breathe.

2. Make sure the lectern feels comfortable. You should, of course, have checked it in advance, but if another speaker has rearranged things (or left his half-empty water glass), now's the time to put things in order. After all, it's *your* podium now.

3. Check the position of the microphone. Again, you should have tested the microphone in advance. Check the switch. If you question the level, just say, "Good morning/afternoon/evening."

   Do not blow into the microphone or tap it. If you have any doubt whether the sound is working properly, simply look at the back of the audience and ask, "Is the sound good?" If it's not, they'll tell you, and you can have the sound person make any adjustments. Whatever you do, don't stand up there staring at the microphone and repeating "Testing, testing, testing."

4. Stand straight and place your weight evenly over both feet. This will help you feel "grounded" and in control of the situation.

5. Take ownership of the space. Mentally *own* that room— every inch of it. Notice the back wall and both side walls.

6. *Look* at the audience before you start to speak. Make them wait a moment. This pause will quiet them and also give you a chance to . . .

7. . . . Breathe!

Now, you're ready to speak.

VOICE

Demosthenes, the Athenian orator, supposedly practiced speaking with a mouthful of pebbles. You don't have to go to such extremes. Check these basics:

- *Rate.* Time yourself with a stopwatch. How many words do you speak in a minute? Most speakers do about 130–140–150 words per minute in English. But rate varies by geography (Northerners in the U.S. talk faster than Southerners) and it varies by age (young people speak faster than older people).

- *Variety.* Can you adjust your pace? Slower to set a particular mood? Faster to create excitement?

- *Emphasis.* Do you emphasize the *right* words?

- *Volume.* Can people hear you? If not, open your mouth more.

- *Rhythm.* Do you vary your sentences?

- *Fillers.* Do you bother your listeners with "uh" and "er" and "ah"?

- *Clarity.* Do you articulate clearly? Don't slur your contractions *(wu'nt* for *wouldn't).* Don't reverse sounds (perscription for prescription). Don't omit sounds (especially common at the ends of long words). Don't add sounds (*acrost* for *across*).

VOICE: GUIDELINES FOR ARTICULATION

1) Don't drop the final -NT.

   a) percent . . . count . . . continent . . . vacant . . . efficient . . . went

   b) can't . . . wouldn't . . . couldn't . . . didn't . . . shouldn't

2) Don't drop the final -LT: "As a result, the plant was never built."

3) Don't drop the final -ST: "We lost the mailing list."

4) Don't drop the final -R: fear . . . door . . . soar . . . offer . . . "core values" . . . "core curriculum"

5) Don't omit the interior -R- sound: party . . . warning . . . start . . . board . . . support . . . market . . . afford . . . large . . . order . . . hard . . . overtime . . . energy . . . "thought leadership"

6) Give -ING its full sound:

   planning . . . starting . . . counting . . . banking . . . managing . . . beginning . . . meeting

It's Not What You Say, It's How You Say It (St. Martin's Press, 2000) offers an extensive section on vocal techniques and other delivery issues. If you're serious about improving your presentation skills, that information will prove invaluable for you.

If you have a speech impediment, I encourage you to get some professional help—it is never too late to improve your voice and feel better about your speech. I have seen marvelous improvements at all ages. Ask your doctor to recommend a speech therapist, or contact local colleges and universities for information on speech clinics. Your local hospital can be an excellent resource and might have a section on their Web site listing speech therapists in your region.

You deserve the right to speak in a way that makes you feel confident and comfortable. If an impediment blocks your rapport with your listeners/audiences, you can change that situation. Reach out to a skilled speech therapist or voice coach. It might be the single most important investment you ever make in yourself. Good luck!

CHECKLIST FOR PAUSES

Skilled presenters know their pauses are as important as their words. Consider these guidelines:

☐ 1) After introductory phrases or clauses:

a) "By the time you meet with the administration, (PAUSE) all of this material will be published."

b) "Even though the board meeting went well, (PAUSE) we can still make some improvements for next year."

☐ 2) Before connecting words ("but," "or," "and," "because," et cetera):

a) "We urged them to revise the proposal, (PAUSE) but they didn't listen to that advice."

b) "Susan usually does a good job; (PAUSE) however, this time her presentation was weak."

☐ 3) When running down a long list of items:

a) "We'll need to review the data . . . (PAUSE) double-check our sources . . . (PAUSE) verify all statistics . . . (PAUSE) seek outside opinion . . . (PAUSE) and do an extra-careful job with proofreading."

b) "We now hold meetings in Toronto . . . (PAUSE) Cleveland . . . (PAUSE) San Francisco . . . (PAUSE) Atlanta . . . (PAUSE) and Seattle.

EYE CONTACT

Good eye contact will do more to help your delivery than anything else.

When you *look* at people, they believe you care about them.

They believe you are sincere. They believe you are honest. How can you go wrong if an audience feels this way about you?

Really *look* at the people in your audience—and look at them as *individuals*. Don't look over their heads or stare at some vague spot in the back of the room. (I've heard these tips offered as advice. I'll be blunt: It's bad advice.)

Don't "sweep" the room with your eyes. Instead, look directly at one person until you finish a thought, then move on to another. You must maintain good eye contact with the audience if you are going to convey sincerity.

Avoid looking repeatedly at the same person. It's best to look at as many individuals as possible in the time allowed. Eye contact will also give you instantaneous feedback.

Does the audience look interested or are they nodding out? If you sense boredom, intensify your eye contact, vary your voice, use body language.

Try not to look around the audience during grammatical pauses (for example, between sentences) because physical movement seems awkward when there's nothing verbal going on.

LECTERNS

Something as basic as using (or not using) a lectern will send a powerful signal to your audience. Most speakers use lecterns most of the time. That's reasonable. After all, lecterns provide a convenient place to put your notes and a glass of water.

Unfortunately, many speakers automatically use lecterns all of the time, and that's too bad. A lectern hides about 70 percent of your body and puts a barrier between you and your audience. Few presentations are improved by barriers.

If you're willing to step away from the lectern (even briefly), you will convey confidence, appear more likable, and become more persuasive. Isn't that worth trying?

In his official farewell address as mayor of New York City,

Rudolph Giuliani stepped away from the lectern at St. Paul's Chapel and walked toward his audience—conveying a deep sense of affection for the people, and eliciting their strong support.

BODY LANGUAGE

Most books on public speaking talk about the importance of gestures. I prefer to talk about the importance of *body language*. It is, of course, important to gesture with your hands if you want to make a point. But it's just as important to speak *with your whole body*.

A raised eyebrow, a smile, a shrug of the shoulders—they all make a statement. If you use them wisely, they can contribute a lot to your speech.

Here's an exercise: Search online for the powerful briefing sessions General H. Norman Schwarzkopf delivered during Operation Desert Shield and Desert Storm. You can learn practical delivery lessons from General Schwarzkopf:

- He stood tall—generally *beside* the lectern (in contrast to many corporate speakers, who hide behind their lecterns for dear life).

- He made bold gestures, and he made them away from the body—easy for all to see.

- He kept direct eye contact with the audience.

- And—most refreshing—he used facial expressions to convey a wide variety of emotions: determination, sympathy, pride, anger, and commitment. (No blank-faced bureaucrat, here.)

It's not necessary (or even advisable) to choreograph your body movements in advance. You'll find that they spring naturally from your message, from your belief in what you're saying. If you put energy and thought and life into your message, your body movements will take good care of themselves. If you *don't*, no amount of hand-waving will help your cause.

As you rehearse and deliver your speech:

- You'll find yourself leaning forward slightly to make a stronger point.

- You'll find yourself smiling when you quote something amusing.

- You'll find yourself nodding slightly when you sense a good response from the audience.

- You'll find yourself shaking your head when you cite something that's offensive or inaccurate.

- You'll find yourself, in short, developing charisma. The more energy you *give* to an audience, the more charisma you will develop. It's an exchange—you give and you get.

A word of caution about gestures: No feeble ones, please. If you raise just a finger to make a point, the audience may not even see the gesture. Raise your whole hand. Raise your whole arm. Make your movements *say* something.

If you have trouble expressing yourself physically, swing your arms in figure eights before you speak. (In privacy, of course.) This big movement will loosen you up.

WHEN YOU FINISH SPEAKING

You've just spoken the last word of your speech. *Be careful.*

Your speech isn't really over. Don't walk away from the podium yet. Hold your position. Look directly at the audience for a few more seconds. Remain in control of the silence just as you remained in control of the speech.

If you wrote a good speech, your final words were strong and memorable. In fact, your ending was probably the best part of the whole speech. Allow it to sink in.

Then, close your folder and walk away from the podium. Walk briskly and confidently—the same way you approached the podium.

When you take your seat, do *not* start talking to the person next to you. Someone else is probably at the podium now, and the audience would think it rude for you to be talking.

Above all, don't whisper things like, "Whew, am I glad *that's* over," or "Could you see how bad my hands were trembling?" I have even seen speakers sit down and roll their eyes and shake their heads—a sure way to detract from an otherwise good speech.

Just sit quietly. Look attentive and confident. There may well be applause. Smile and look pleased to be there. It would seem unnatural to act any other way.

Some speakers—those with a lot at stake—even plan their applause. They make sure that staff members attend the speech—not sitting together, but spread throughout the audience. When these people start to applaud, they produce a ripple effect. Voila! A standing ovation!

NERVOUSNESS

"I'm afraid I'll be nervous." That's a common feeling, and in some ways it's healthy. It shows you care about getting your message across to the audience. You really *do* want to look and sound good.

But it's important to understand what nervousness is. Nervousness is simply *energy*. If you channel that energy, you can turn it into a positive force. You can make it work for you. You can use the extra energy to your advantage.

But if you allow that energy to go unchecked—if you allow *it* to control *you*—then you're going to have problems. A dry mouth, perhaps, or a cracking voice. Lots of rocking back and forth on your feet, or lots of "uh's" and "um's." Maybe even forgetfulness.

How can you channel your nervous energy? By taking the

advice that appears in this chapter. Learn to direct your extra energy into eye contact, body language, and vocal enthusiasm. These physical activities provide an outlet for your nervousness. They offer a way to use up some of that extra energy.

What's more, good eye contact, strong body language, and vocal enthusiasm will build your *confidence*. It's hard to feel insecure when you look directly at your listeners and see the responsiveness in their faces.

PRE-SPEECH TRICKS TO PREVENT NERVOUSNESS

There are tricks to every trade, and public speaking is no exception. Consider what professional speakers do to keep their nervousness in check.

Start by addressing any nervousness with your doctor or dentist. Medical professionals can provide sound oversight. (Dentists, in particular, are keenly aware of nervousness or stress that's expressed as jaw clenching or teeth grinding.)

Here are a few practical exercises that have helped other speakers:

- *Try physical exercises.* Just before you speak, go off by yourself (to the restroom or to a quiet corner) and concentrate on the part of your body that feels most tense. Your face? Your hands? Your stomach? Deliberately tighten that part even more, then let go. You will feel an enormous sense of relief. Repeat this a few times.

- Slowly drop your head. Let your cheek muscles go loose and let your mouth go slack.

- Make funny faces. Puff up your cheeks, then let the air escape. Or open your mouth and your eyes wide, then close them tightly. Alternate a few times. Yawn a few times to loosen your jaw and your mucous membranes.

- Pretend you're an opera singer. Try "mi, mi, mi" a few times. Wave your arms as you do it.

- *Try mental exercises.* Picture something that's given you pleasant memories: sailing on a blue-green ocean; swimming in a mountain lake; or walking on a beach and feeling the sand between your toes. (Water often has a calming effect on people.)

- *Try a rational approach.* Say to yourself, "I'm prepared. I know what I'm talking about." Or, "I've spent a year working on this project. Nobody knows as much about this project as I do." Or, "I'm glad I can talk to these people. It will help my career." I know someone who repeats to herself, "This is better than death, this is better than death." That may sound extreme, but it works for her—and she's right. Giving a speech *is* better than death.

  If you're scared to give a speech, try to think of something that's *really* frightening to you. The speech should seem appealing by comparison.

- *Try a test run.* Visualize exactly what will happen after you're introduced. You'll get out of your chair; you'll hold the folder in your left hand; you'll walk confidently across the stage; you'll hold your head high; you'll look directly at the person who introduced you; you'll shake his or her hand; you'll . . . *If you see yourself as confident and successful in your mental test run, you'll be confident and successful in your delivery.*

Above all, never *say* that you're nervous. *Never.* If you do, you'll make yourself more nervous, and you'll make the audience nervous, too.

DURING-THE-SPEECH TRICKS TO
OVERCOME NERVOUSNESS

Okay. You've prepared your speech carefully. You've done the pre-speech exercises. Now you're at the podium and—can that be?—your mouth goes a little dry.

Don't panic. Just intensify your eye contact. Looking at the audience will take away your self-preoccupation and reduce the dryness.

Persistent dryness? Help yourself to the glass of water that you've wisely placed at the lectern. Don't be embarrassed. Say to yourself, "It's my speech, and I can drink water if I want to."

Other minitraumas?

- *Sweat rolling off your forehead.* Wipe it away with the big cotton handkerchief that you also placed at the lectern. Don't hesitate to really *wipe*. Little dabs are ineffectual, and you'll have to dab repeatedly. Do it right the first time, and get it over with. Also, avoid using tissues. They can shred and get stuck on your face—not a terribly impressive sight.

- *A quavery voice.* Pause. Intensify your eye contact. Focus on *them*. Then lower your pitch and control your breath as you begin to speak. Concentrate on speaking distinctly and slowly.

- *Shaking hands.* Take heart. The audience probably can't see your trembling hands, but if it makes you self-conscious or distracts your concentration, then use some body movement to diffuse that nervous energy. Change your foot position. Step forward as you make a point. Lean toward the audience. Move your arms. Do something to help your body burn off that nervousness. (If your body stays stuck in a frozen position, your shaking will only grow worse.)

- *A pounding heart.* No, the audience *cannot* see the rising and falling of your chest. If you have concerns, ask your doctor.

- *Throat clearing.* If you have to cough, cough—away from the microphone. Drink some water, or pop a piece of a cough drop into your mouth. Again, the well-prepared speaker has a cough drop handy at all times—unwrapped, smacked into tiny slivers, ready to use.

- *Runny nose, watery eyes.* Bright lights can trigger these responses. Simply pause, say "Excuse me," blow your nose or wipe your eyes, and get on with it. Don't make a big deal over it by apologizing. A simple "Excuse me" is just fine.

- *Nausea.* You come down with some virus before your speech and you're afraid of throwing up in the middle of your presentation. Don't worry needlessly. Ask your doctor for advice.

  For actors, the show must always go on, even with serious infections. More than one actor has placed a trash can backstage so he could throw up between acts.

  But *you* are not an actor. Why infect everyone else? If you are terribly ill—as opposed to being just mildly nervous—cancel your engagement. Since you've prepared a complete manuscript, perhaps a colleague could substitute for you. If substitution is not possible, offer to speak at a later date.

- *Burping.* Some people feel they have to burp when they get nervous. If you are one of these people, do plenty of physical relaxation exercises before you speak. Don't drink any carbonated beverages that day, and eat only a light lunch. Keep lunchtime quiet by eating alone. Avoid talking while eating.

- *Fumbled words.* Professional speakers, radio announcers, and television anchors fumble words fairly often. Someone once introduced President Reagan with this slip of the tongue: "Everyone who is for abortion was at one time a feces [sic]." So, why should *you* expect to be perfect?

If it's a minor fumble, just ignore it and keep going. If it's a big one, fix it. Simply repeat the correct word—with a smile, to show you're human.

Continue with your speech, but slow down a little bit. Once you've had a slip of the tongue, chances are high you'll have another. A fumble is a symptom that you're focusing more on yourself than on your message. Relax and slow down.

- *Forgetfulness.* Some people look at an audience and forget what they want to say. Aren't you glad you made the effort to prepare a well-written manuscript? It's all right there, so you have one less thing to worry about.

HECKLERS

As a goose is not frightened by cackling nor a sheep
by bleating, so let not the clamor of a senseless
multitude alarm you.

—EPICTETUS

Hecklers tend to exist only in the bad dreams of speakers. They almost never pose real-life problems. However, if you are in the middle of your speech and you see someone waving an arm at you, then you need real-life help—and fast.

First of all, stay calm. Hecklers are like people who make obscene telephone calls. They just love to upset you. If you stay calm, you destroy their pleasure. If you stay calm, you also stay in control.

Ignore the hand that's waving in the air and keep right on speaking. It takes a lot of energy to wave a hand in the air, and the person will probably grow tired and give up. (Try waving your hand in the air for a few minutes, and you'll see what I mean.)

If you hear a voice? Stop speaking, remain calm, and ask the person to hold the question until after your speech. Be polite but firm. The audience will respect your approach and the person will most likely respect your request. Proceed with your speech.

If the person gets louder, you should *not* continue. Look instead at the person who organized this speaking engagement. If you're lucky, that person will come to your aid and quiet the heckler or escort him out of the room.

If not, speak to the heckler again. Say, "As I said before, I'll be glad to answer all questions *after* my speech." By now, your patience and professionalism should have earned the respect—and sympathy—of the rest of the audience.

If the heckling worsens, confront the person. Say, "Everyone here knows I'm *(name)* and I'm from the *(name)* company. Could you tell us who *you* are?" Hecklers, like obscene phone callers, prefer to remain anonymous.

If the tirade continues, you will have to count on the audience for their support. Stop speaking, and step back just a few inches from the lectern. Stand tall. Be strong, firm, silent. Let the event's organizers put pressure on the heckler to shut up or leave.

After all, *you* are the invited speaker, not the heckler. You shouldn't have to justify your presence. You have a right to be treated fairly and to get your message across.

In the one in a million case where an audience isn't willing to support your basic rights, then don't waste your time trying to speak to them. Leave—with dignity.

EMBARRASSING GLITCHES

When reviewing your speech manuscript, pay special attention to noun/verb confusions. Certain words can serve either as a noun or a verb, depending on which syllable you stress.

Consider: *produce, project, reject,* and *console.* When you put the emphasis on the first syllable, they're all nouns. ("We'll need three months to complete this *project.*") If you accent the second syllable, those same words become verbs. ("Here's how we *project* our expenses.")

If you mistakenly accent the wrong syllable, you'll look like you're "reading" your speech for the first time—which seriously undercuts your authority as a speaker. Rehearse.

Many years ago, I interviewed Maggie Kuhn, founder of the Gray Panthers. The following caution comes from this remarkable activist: "When you least expect it, someone may actually listen to what you have to say."

My advice: When they're listening, make sure you sound good.

TWELVE

MEDIA AND SOCIAL MEDIA

*How can you squander even one more day not
taking advantage of the greatest shifts of our genera-
tion? How dare you settle for less when the world
has made it so easy for you to be remarkable?*
−SETH GODIN, BESTSELLING AUTHOR

Your speech probably won't merit global TV news coverage but
that's okay. You have lots of other ways to get good attention for
your messages.

Start small and work your way up the publicity scale.

Begin with the basics and do as much as your budget and your
time will allow—and, yes, as much as your *material* will allow.

Face it, not all speeches are newsworthy. If you expect media
attention for a routine speech, you will be disappointed.

Much clamors for our attention, and much fails to get our
attention. As Pete Cushmore, founder of Mashable, put it:

We're living at a time when attention is the new currency.
With hundreds of TV channels, billions of Web sites, pod-
casts, radio shows, music downloads and social networking,
our attention is more fragmented than ever before.

So, with all the content distractions, how can you get good
publicity for your speech? Here are sixteen suggestions:

1. *Give it a catchy title.* Come up with titles that *beg* to be quoted.

    I have a hobby: For many years, I've collected samples of speech titles that were noted, verbatim, in *The New York Times* and other news forums. What have I learned from this? I've learned that when you use a clever, creative, zippy title— something that just begs to be quoted—it's more likely to get quoted. I've also learned that when speakers use boring titles like "Opportunities and Challenges in the Energy Industry," or "Remarks on Public Housing Issues," those titles never get quoted. Never.

    So, it behooves all of us to come up with good titles for our presentations.

    This 2013 title from an Air Force speech certainly caught my attention: "I Am Duct Tape." Given by Colonel Darrell Young, 934th Airlift Wing commander, at an AF volunteer recognition dinner in Minneapolis, this marvelous little speech offers a riff on one obscure word: "ductility." Don't know what the word "ductility" means? Until I read the speech, I didn't know either! But that's what clever titles do. They pull us in. We learn new things, and we also see old things in new ways.

    Need ideas? Try variations on the titles of popular movies, books, and songs. Do something humorous with the date. Paraphrase the title you used at last year's meeting. Do a creative take-off on the official conference theme. Be specific. Be graphic. Be irreverent if you want. Just don't be boring.

2. *Announce pubic speeches on LinkedIn.* One or two months before your speech, post a "Save the date" notice. I regularly do this when I'm invited to speak at conferences. Sure enough, at the event, an attendee will come up to me and say, "I saw the notice on LinkedIn. Glad I could come."

3. *About two weeks prior to your presentation, provide some "teaser material" to share with your regular LinkedIn groups.* Let them know about your topic, and share a few quotable tidbits that will catch their attention. Invite them to stop by your presentation and introduce themselves. *Remember:* The emphasis in the term "social media" goes on the word "social." The whole purpose is to connect people. The more sociable you are, the more successful you'll be.

4. *Offer copies of your remarks to the audience.* If you're using PowerPoint, offer to e-mail that material to anyone who's interested. Then keep your word, and e-mail the presentation as soon as possible—ideally within twenty-four hours, at least within forty-eight hours. Follow-through makes a big impression. Prompt follow through makes an even bigger impression.

   How do I know this? Because I frequently speak to professional associations (the International Association of Business Communicators and the American Society of Journalists and Authors are a couple of examples), and I always offer to send follow-up materials. Invariably audiences will tell me, "Thank you so much for the follow-through, Joan! Lots of speakers promise to send us material, but they never do."

   Get a multiplier effect by encouraging the audience to share your materials. In the industrial age, people were only as strong as their weakest link. But in the social media age, people are as strong as the number and quality of their shares. Who "likes" your content? Who provides thoughtful comments about your online material?

   A caution is in order here. Let your audience know upfront that you're happy to provide them with a full copy of your presentation. Don't make them sit there feverishly taking notes for twenty minutes before you tell them you'll be providing an electronic summary. I've seen many speakers make this mistake, and the results have not been pretty. Audiences resent taking copious notes only to learn later that their efforts were needless.

One practical suggestion: Have assistants posted at the doors as the audience leaves to collect business cards from any interested attendees. This will spare you from having to deal with hordes of people descending on you at the lectern with their various requests.

I'm not kidding about the chaos that can occur at a podium.

Beware of after-speech hordes. When the governor of the People's Bank of China, Zhou Xiaochuan, finished speaking at the Boao Forum in 2012, he was set upon by journalists hoping to catch one more quotable word—and one reporter even fell off the stage in all the hoopla.

In another case, at a professional conference, I watched a fellow panelist try to fend off attendees trying to network after his presentation. He stepped backward in an effect to escape and fell off the three-foot platform.

So, beware of after-speech hordes.

For that matter, beware of *during-speech* hordes. I once attended a conference in New York City where a speaker mentioned he brought samples of his product to give away but said he was worried he hadn't brought enough. At this point, I watched in amazement as many in the audience stood up, climbed over seats, and interrupted the speaker in their quest to snag a free sample. (You can't make this stuff up.)

5. *Send an advance copy of the speech to the trade publication that serves your business.* Make the editor's work easier:

- Be sure the speech is easy to read, with short paragraphs and wide margins.

- Add subheads to catch the editor's attention.

- Use color blocks to highlight a couple of quotable phrases in the speech—phrases the editor can pull out and use in a caption or headline or call-out.

- Attach a one-paragraph summary. This summary may be the only thing the editor bothers to read, so make it good. Include an impressive statistic or a memorable quote or an interesting example—anything that will quickly grab an editor's attention.

6. *Polish your Web site.* Potential audience members will no doubt visit your Web site to check your background. Make sure your site is mobile-friendly and up-to-date. Repeat key messages throughout your site. (Take inspiration from Thomas Watson, who built IBM. He was famous for the slogan THINK, which he plastered everywhere: on walls, on stationery, at home. Let that be a model for a speaker's messages.) Above all, don't let your Web site visitors discover announcements that went out of date three months ago.

7. *Connect with bloggers who write about your field.* Think in terms of relationship-building. Comment on their blogs. "Like" their blogs. Share their blogs. Offer suggestions for topics. Offer introductions to people in your network. Then, when you give an interesting presentation, it's perfectly natural for you to share this news.

8. *Send a copy to nearby colleges and universities.*

- The career office may want to share a link with students who apply to your company.

- The appropriate department may want to present your ideas in class. [Note: Too few speakers reach out to nearby colleges and universities. That's a real loss, because if professors note parts of your speech in their classes or in their writings, you benefit from multiplier effects.]

9. *Send a notice of your speech to your alma mater.* Colleges and universities are enormously proud of their alumni. If you're invited to speak at a major conference, they'll be proud of you, too. They might invite you back to campus to give a lecture, or they might do a feature on you and your work in the alumni magazine. Do not overlook these possibilities. Keep in touch with other alums through LinkedIn groups.

10. *Contact local newspapers, local radio shows, or TV stations.* Make your releases short and snappy. Don't think "corporate," think "newsworthy, interesting, or important." Put yourself in the shoes of an editor or a news director and ask, "What kind of press release would I like to receive?" The universal answer: "The kind that makes my work easier."

   For newspapers: Give them a good lead, something they can use "as is." Editors aren't looking for more work. They're looking for good stories to make their work easier. Give them a good lead, and they may give you good coverage.

   For radio and TV: Give them three or four short sentences written for the ear and ready to deliver on the air. *Remember:* News directors receive many press releases each day. It's human nature for them to use the ones that are "ready to go"—that don't require extensive research and rewriting.

   If you sense interest, offer written backup material. Include any recent publications. A book or a magazine feature will increase your credibility. For TV shows, offer to provide visuals—photos, footage, small-scale models, posters, charts, even documents that you can show as you make your point.

   Television is a highly visual medium. If you offer to show things to the viewers, you will stand a better chance of getting on the show.

11. *Share the speech with your local chamber of commerce.* They might excerpt a portion on their Web site. Offer to serve as a resource. Encourage Web site visitors to write to you with any questions they might have. Provide answers graciously. Charles Darwin wasn't thinking about social media when he wrote, "In the long history of humankind . . . those who learned to collaborate and improvise most effectively have prevailed." But his observation sums up the online culture of sharing and collaborating.

12. *Ask the host organization to publicize your appearance.* They have a vested interest in the success of your speech, so get them involved. Make sure they announce your appearance well in advance. After the speech is over, ask them to provide a link on their Web site—so members who missed your live presentation can at least benefit from reading it online.

13. *Blog.* If you don't already have a blog, start one. The more speeches you give, the bigger your platform will grow—and the more people who can follow your blog.

14. *Don't overlook your business cards.* The old-fashioned business card serves an important message function. Don't just put your contact info on the front and let the back of the card remain empty. Empty gets you nothing.

    Instead, turn your business card into a marketing tool simply by creating relevant copy for both sides. What could you put on the back? Titles of recent speeches . . . a list of impressive audiences . . . a blurb recommending you as a speaker . . . a stunning statistic from one of your presentations . . . an endorsement of your work . . . honors you have received . . . magazines where you have been published.

    Consider putting a question on the back of your business card. Make it a question that will require the recipient to think about you and your key message.

    As a speechwriter and speech coach, I often go onsite to

help organizations create more cost-effective presentations. So, to keep my message top-of-mind with those audiences, I give out business cards with this copy on the back:

HOW MUCH DO POOR PRESENTATIONS COST YOUR ORGANIZATION?

Add up all the preparation time, the travel expenses,
the combined work hours lost by attendees.
Then add in your opportunity costs.
Fix your presentation drain . . . *now*.

15. *Think global.* While your audience might be local, your topic might be global. Make a concerted effort to connect with audiences on all continents via LinkedIn. Attract an international Facebook following. (Right now, only about 10–15 percent of people's friends on Facebook come from other countries.) The simple truth is: most topics cross borders. Green initiatives, domestic violence, teenage health, gun safety, literacy . . . you could address any of these topics locally and yet attract media attention for your message internationally.

16. *Increase the number of your LinkedIn contacts.* Why have 135 good contacts when you can (with a little bit of effort) have 700 good contacts? The more people who know about you and your speeches, the better the buzz.

Make the most of your speech. After all, you worked hard to prepare it. Now, make it work hard *for you*.

THIRTEEN

INTERNATIONAL SPEECHES

Az me hunt iber di planken, bakumt men andereh
gedanken.
[If you cross over the fence, you acquire other ideas.]
–YIDDISH PROVERB

The globalization of business has brought many changes—not the least of which is a need to communicate with international audiences.

A South American manufacturer is asked to speak in Moscow, Japanese executives prepare for an important presentation in California, a German banker needs to address a group of international bankers meeting in London, a U.S. accountant must speak at a professional women's conference in France, an entrepreneur wants to meet with audiences around the world to promote his products. These are now common speaking assignments.

Unfortunately, few speakers have adequate experience with international audiences, and they bring many anxieties to the podium:

- What are the distinctive demands of this foreign audience?

- How can I be sure my message is getting across?

- What should I do to avoid cross-cultural gaffes?

- Will humor work across language barriers?

- How can I show respect for my hosts?

- How can I express pride in my own cultural heritage?

The following examples will show how other leaders have dealt with international speaking assignments. Perhaps you can gain some ideas by listening to their techniques.

HOW TO GET YOUR MESSAGE ACROSS IN ANY LANGUAGE

USE RHETORICAL PHRASING TO CREATE A DELIVERY WITH MORE IMPACT

Canadian prime minister Stephen Harper used distinctive phrasing when he delivered his 2012 Remembrance Day remarks in Hong Kong:

On this day, in such places of quiet rest for the fallen, and beside monuments to their sacrifice, we gather in the old Act of Remembrance.

We recite the old words, speak sometimes of old friends or forebears who, to our lasting benefit and their everlasting glory, served our country to the full.

And we call with reasonable hope upon the Ancient of Days that He will deal mercifully with their eternal souls.

Age shall not weary them, nor the years condemn.

It is a simple truth.

For indeed, they shall grow not old, as we that are left grow old.

Yet it is also a prayer that we may answer.

For it lies within each one of us to remember the dead as they once were.

MAKE IT TIMELY

When former president Jimmy Carter delivered a speech at the University of Havana in 2002, he gained media attention as the first U.S. president to visit Cuba since Fidel Castro took power back in 1959.

Speaking in Spanish and using a prepared text, Carter broke through four decades of mistrust with these words: "It is time for us to change our relationship and the way we think and talk about each other."

SHOW COMMON INTERESTS

When Prime Minister Jens Stoltenberg of Norway spoke at a business seminar in Tokyo in 2012, he opened with these lines:

> In geographical distance, Japan and Norway are far apart. But we have close cooperation in a large number of areas.
>
> We share common values and are both strong defenders of democracy and human rights. We work closely together on many important international issues—maternal and child health and UN reform, to mention a few.
>
> And we are working together to address today's greatest challenge, the threat of climate change.

USE REPETITION

Repetition is a stylistic device that makes any speech more memorable. But with international speeches, repetition does more than add style. It enhances comprehension. It increases the ability of audiences from different backgrounds, with different languages, to grasp your message.

When Slovakian president Ivan Gašparovič delivered a 2012

speech at the UN General Assembly in New York, he opened with these effective lines:

> Conflicts do not stop at the borders. The world we live in is so much intertwined that every problem is a problem of all of us, every threat is a threat to all of us, but every success will also bring benefits to all of us.

EXPRESS YOUR PLEASURE AT THE PRIVILEGE OF ADDRESSING THIS FOREIGN AUDIENCE

As the chairman of the Fiat Group, Giovanni Agnelli was invited to give the annual Romanes Lecture at Oxford University in England. (The Romanes invitation goes to a distinguished figure from the arts, science, or literature. None other than William Gladstone gave the first lecture in 1892).

Agnelli acknowledged the cross-cultural honor this way:

> Over the past hundred years, the Romanes Lecture has been given by some of Britain's most illustrious men and women. I believe this is the first time that an Italian has been invited to take the platform at this prestigious event, and I am most grateful to the chancellor and the University of Oxford authorities for according me the honour.
>
> However, I should perhaps warn you that I am an industrialist, *not* an academic, and so I hope you will not expect me to give you a lecture in the strict sense of the word. What I would like to do instead is to discuss a subject currently of major public interest: *What is Europe?*

RE-CREATE A TIME AND PLACE

It's always useful to give an audience a sense of time and place, but with international audiences this becomes more critical. If the audience needs some background information to put your message in perspective, give it to them.

Marie Curie did exactly this when she gave a remarkable address at Vassar College in 1921 about the discovery of radium. Since her speech was given more than twenty years after the actual discovery, Madame Curie took a few moments up front to set the stage:

> I could tell you many things about radium and radioactivity and it would take a long time. But as we can not do that, I shall only give you a short account of my early work about radium.
>
> Radium is no more a baby, it is more than twenty years old, but the conditions of the discovery were somewhat peculiar, and so it is always of interest to remember them and to explain them.
>
> We must go back to the year 1897. Professor Curie and I worked at that time in the laboratory of the school of Physics and Chemistry where Professor Curie held his lectures. . . .

With those few well-chosen words, Marie Curie took that audience back two decades to the lab where it all happened.

USE A THEME THAT UNITES YOUR SPEAKERS AND THEIR TOPICS

In 2012, the Salvation Army held its Europe Congress in Prague. What united 1,300 Salvationists coming from thirty countries? The strong theme: "Forward! In Confidence, Unity, and Power."

The sessions centered around the Salvation Army's International Vision (expressed in a triad): "One Army, One Mission, One Message."

The most compelling statistic at the conference? Commissioner Robert Street held up a piece of the Berlin Wall—a reminder

that, until recent years, The Salvation Army was totally pro-
scribed in twelve European countries where it now operates.

BE VIVID

When newly elected Brazilian president Fernando Collor de Mello
evaluated the economic situation in his country, he used highly
visual details that would make a powerful impression in *any*
language:

> I am driving a packed bus at 150 kilometers per hour, headed
> for a cliff. Either we put on the brakes and some people get a
> little bruised up, or we go over the edge and we all die.

CITE LONG-STANDING FRIENDSHIPS

When Abdullah II, His Majesty, King of Jordan, spoke to the
Houses of Parliament of the United Kingdom of Great Britain and
Northern Ireland, he was the first head of state from the Arab
Middle East to address those parliamentary members. He began
by recalling his late father, His Majesty King Hussein, who "led
the way as a peace-maker and voice of moderation in the Middle
East. I am delighted to see so many of his friends here today."

HONOR THE REAL MEANING OF AN ANNIVERSARY

In 2009, at the European Parliament in Brussels, Václav Havel
delivered a speech to commemorate the twentieth anniversary of
the fall of the Iron Curtain in Central and Eastern Europe. The
former Czech president and freedom fighter prodded his audience with these words:

> Europe's rich spiritual and cultural history—combining
> elements of Antiquity, Judaism, Christianity, Islam, the

Renaissance, and the Enlightenment—has created an array
of indisputable values, to which the European Union pays
lip service, but which it often regards simply as pretty pack-
aging for the things that really matter. But aren't these values
what really matter, and are not they, on the contrary, what
give direction to all the rest?

A personal note:
When I was in Prague for New Year's Day 2013, I saw how much
Václav Havel's words still resonate with the Czech people. Thousands of people brought flowers and lit candles to place by the
monument honoring Havel. Many stopped for a quiet moment of
reflection.

EMPHASIZE WHAT ALL FAMILIES SHARE

When First Lady Eleanor Roosevelt spoke on V-J Day, she expressed
sensitivity to all the families who suffered during World War II:

> The day for which the people of the world have prayed is here
> at last . . . . For the happy wives and mothers of my own coun-
> try and of the world, my heart rejoices today, but I cannot
> forget that to many this moment only adds a poignancy to their
> grief. All women—wives and mothers, sisters or sweethearts—
> who have had men involved in this conflict, know what it is
> to live with fear as a constant companion.

DEFINE MATTERS IN YOUR OWN TERMS

When President Gerald Ford spoke in Helsinki back in 1965, he
used this definition of peace to resonate with a worldwide audience: "Peace is a process requiring mutual restraint and practical
arrangements."

ABOVE ALL . . . REMEMBER THAT IT'S NEVER TOO LATE TO SPEAK UP

When British prime minister David Cameron entered Parliament to speak in January 2013, he didn't just get an enthusiastic response to his message on the relationship between Britain and the European Union. He got the satisfaction that comes from finally completing a long-held goal. As Mr. Cameron himself described it, "I've been waiting to give this speech for twenty years."

Most of us won't have to wait twenty years to speak our minds on an issue, but the lesson still applies: There's always a way (and a time) to say what you really want to say.

HOW TO USE A TRANSLATOR OR INTERPRETER

> *If I want to sell you something, then I speak in your language.* Aber wenn Sie mir 'was verkaufen wollen, dann sollen Sie meine Sprache können. *[But if you want to sell me something, then you ought to be able to speak my language.]*
>
> –HELMUT KOHL,
> FORMER CHANCELLOR OF GERMANY

When Joseph Pulitzer published the *New York World* newspaper at the turn of the century, he got the bizarre idea to take his advertising campaign beyond the earth and extend it to the entire *universe*. How? By erecting an enormous advertising sign in New Jersey that would be visible on Mars. He abandoned his plan only when an associate asked, "What language would we print it in?"

What language, indeed?

Of course, most translation assignments prove a little more mundane than Mr. Pulitzer's, but even the most ordinary of interpretation is demanding. For starters, let's address the distinction between translators and interpreters.

Translators work with *written* language—for example, rewriting the manuscript of an English speech into Japanese.

Interpreters work with *spoken* language. Interpreters often do their work live: As the speaker delivers in German, the interpreter simultaneously offers the remarks to the U.S. audience in English.

Make no mistake: There's a huge difference between someone who happens to speak a foreign language, and someone who has the highly developed skills to serve as an interpreter or a translator in important business dealings.

Interpretation and translation clearly demand a professional, and you will get only what you pay for.

For more than a decade, I have provided speaker coaching for an international organization. I've worked with their speakers from around the world, including Japan, Brazil, Korea, Portugal, and Taiwan. Sometimes, they present in English, but if their English skills are not strong enough, then they present in their native languages. In these cases, I work very closely with interpreters and translators. Over the years, I have come to appreciate the full value of their skills. When you are fortunate enough to work with a great translator or interpreter, be generous with your thank-yous. And be sure to get their business card.

If *you* are giving a speech to an audience that speaks another language, how can you find an interpreter who's adequately skilled for *your* purposes? Try asking these practical questions when interviewing prospective interpreters:

- "Where were you trained?"

- "What are the credentials of your schools/teachers?"

- "What was the nature of your training?" (In other words, German literature versus business German.)

- "How often do you work as an interpreter?" (Yes, foreign language skills *do* get rusty.)

- "Did you ever *live* in this foreign country?"

- "What were your last three interpreting assignments?" (Ask for specific details: lengths of assignments, types of material, the clients' fields, any unusual circumstances, et cetera.)

- "Have you ever served as an interpreter within my particular industry?" (This is a critical point. Each business has its own lingo, its own buzz words. You want someone who can translate your distinctive terminology like an insider.)

In addition, ask yourself some questions:

- "Do I feel comfortable with this interpreter?" (Rapport is an important factor. After all, you'll need to place a great deal of trust in your interpreter—and you want to do it with confidence.)

- "Will this person represent me well, in an attractive, well-groomed manner?" (Look at it this way: In the eyes of the audience, your interpreter is literally a stand-in for *you*.)

Here's a final caveat about using interpreters, straight from the mouth of President Reagan.

In his February 1988 remarks to the National Governors' Association, President Reagan included this bit of self-deprecating humor about the pitfalls of speaking to a foreign audience:

As you know, I recently visited Mexico to meet with President De La Madrid. And I was reminded of when I was governor of California and was asked by the then-president to go down and represent him. . . .

On this first visit to Mexico, I gave a speech to a rather large audience and then sat down to rather unenthusiastic and scattered applause. I was embarrassed and tried to cover all of that, because what made it worse was that the next speaker up was speaking in Spanish, which I didn't understand, but he was getting interrupted virtually every line with most enthusiastic applause.

So, I started clapping before anyone else and longer than anyone else until our ambassador learned over and said to me, "I wouldn't do that if I were you. He's interpreting your speech."

THE FINISHING TOUCHES

Consider all of the "little things" you can do to give your international speeches a special flair.

- When H. Norman Schwarzkopf was made an honorary member of the French Foreign Legion at a ceremony near Marseilles, he flattered his audience by delivering his most powerful line in French. Speaking directly to the Foreign Legion officers, he used his best French accent to offer his heartfelt praise: "Your men are great."

- When Steve Harlan, as vice chairman, international, of KPMG, addressed the benefits of free trade with Mexico, he concluded with an old Mexican proverb. First, he delivered the proverb in its original Spanish, *"El que adelante no mira, atrás se queda."* Then, he paused a moment and offered its English translation, "He who doesn't look ahead, stays behind." By offering the foreign proverb in both languages, he created a more dramatic rapport with his international audience.

- In his historic visit to Cuba at the age of seventy-seven, Pope John Paul II delivered his homily in Spanish—and the crowds responded enthusiastically. This was the first visit of a successor to St. Peter to the nation of Cuba. In consideration of his historic visit, the Cuban government reestablished Christmas as a public holiday—even if only for that year (1997). The sounds of maracas and drums set to Roman Catholic prayers filled the air—a reminder that music is truly the international language.

- In 2011, Queen Elizabeth visited Ireland—the first such visit by a British monarch since Irish independence. At a state banquet, she caught everyone by surprise by suddenly speaking in Gaelic. No one could have been more surprised than the president of Ireland, who mouthed "Wow." Wow, indeed.

FOURTEEN

SPEAKERS BUREAUS

It is generally better to deal by speech than by letter.
—FRANCIS BACON,
LORD CHANCELLOR OF ENGLAND

Do these situations sound familiar?

- You're an administrator at a hospital, you've just expanded your outpatient services, and you'd like more people to know about your new facilities. What's the best way to reach potential patients?

- You're the owner of a small business, and you'd like to generate positive attention for your services. Unfortunately, you don't have the budget to do an advertising campaign or hire a public relations firm. What can you tell the community about your business that will attract new customers?

- You're a manager at an electric utility, and customers are worried about the risks of transmission lines. How can you convince the community that your operations are safe?

- You're a branch manager at a bank, and you need to pursue new customers more aggressively. How can you persuade customers to use the wide spectrum of financial services you offer?

- You're active in a local environmental group, and you'd like to take your messages to a wide range of audiences—from public schools to colleges, from senior centers to business groups.

Consider setting up your own *speakers bureau*. A speakers bureau is an *organized* effort to communicate a company's message to specific target groups—perhaps to the Rotary, or to the chamber of commerce . . . to women's groups, men's clubs, or school groups . . . to affinity groups or political clubs.

Organizations large and small are finding that speakers bureaus are an effective, low-cost way to reach a variety of civic, business, professional, social, and educational organizations—in short, to present their message to important constituencies within their communities.

Pharmaceutical companies, utilities, oil companies, banks, and hospitals are just a few of the large corporations that have benefited by running effective speakers bureaus.

But you don't have to be a huge organization to benefit. Local charities, churches, faith groups, small family-run businesses . . . they can all leverage the power of a speakers bureau. Self-employed individuals—accountants, attorneys, chiropractors, veterinarians, consultants, landscapers, fitness coaches, therapists, freelance writers, and artisans, to name a few—can benefit enormously from a public speaking presence. Why? Without the advantage of a big PR or advertising budget, solopreneurs must compete on the basis of their message. When their message is strong, they can have as much podium clout as anyone else.

If you'd like to set up a brand-new speakers bureau for your organization . . . if you'd like to pump some life into an inactive, ineffective bureau . . . or if you'd simply like to give speeches that will bring attention to your own business . . . read on. These guidelines should help.

MEMBERSHIP

Who can become a member of your speakers bureau? Well, if you're a solopreneur, it pretty much comes down to you: You'd be the speaker, representing your own business.

But if you work in a large organization, you have many choices. Consider who might be eligible to speak.

- Any current employee?

- Either part-time or full-time?

- Both union and management?

- From entry-level to upper management?

- How about the company's retirees? (They typically know the company well, are quite aware of industry issues, have time to donate, enjoy sharing their expertise, and can prove quite credible to audiences.)

SIZE

How large should you make your bureau? Answer: Only as large as you can manage.

After all, what's the sense in having twenty members listed with your speakers bureau if you can't book enough speaking engagements to keep them all involved, or if you can't find enough time to supervise each speaker?

A better option: Keep the bureau small, and do a more effective job of managing each speaker's special talents.

TRAINING

Your speakers will be only as good as the training they get. So, decide up front *how* you wish to train them, and *how often.*

Again, what's the use of having twenty members in your bureau if you can't get the budget to train all of them effectively?

Much smarter:
Match the size of your membership to your training budget. If you can get only enough money to train five members each year, then be realistic. Limit the size of your bureau to that number. Better to train five members well than to train twenty members poorly. Don't try to save money and/or time by skipping training sessions—that's no bargain.

PAYMENT/BENEFITS

Wise speakers bureaus generally avoid monetary payment because there are too many variables and too many pitfalls. After all, should a mediocre speaker get the same fee as a terrific speaker? Would evening or weekend speeches demand higher rates?

Perhaps most important, "paid" speakers won't have as much credibility with an audience as volunteers who speak from personal commitment. Audiences are quick to spot a "hired gun"—and often respond accordingly.

A smarter choice:
Offer your speakers *other* forms of compensation. After members have given a significant number of speeches, consider offering some extra vacation time, a makeover session at a local salon (which, by the way, will improve their podium appearance), or the opportunity to take advanced courses in presentation skills. Whatever your choice, let your speakers know their efforts are appreciated. Equally important, let them know their speaking efforts will be recognized in upcoming performance reviews.

You'll also need to address the whole issue of expense accounts. Decide *in advance* if you'll reimburse your speakers for taxi fares, car mileage, and restaurant meals. Just as important, decide *in advance* what your limits will be. Otherwise, you might find yourself paying speakers too much money to dine in fancy restaurants en route to their engagements.

RECOGNITION/MOTIVATION

People often say that motivation doesn't last. Well, neither does bathing—that's why we recommend it daily.
–ZIG ZIGLAR, AUTHOR, SALESMAN,
AND MOTIVATIONAL SPEAKER

Let's face it: When employees give up a Saturday afternoon to speak at a community event on the company's behalf, when they trudge out in a snowstorm to honor a speaking engagement at the chamber of commerce, or when they drop what they're doing to fill in as a last-minute speaker at the Rotary . . . well, don't you think they deserve some special recognition?

Here are some ideas:

- Host an annual breakfast, luncheon, or dinner for the bureau's members. Let your budget determine the meal and the restaurant you choose. *Remember*: A first-rate breakfast is more luxurious than a third-rate dinner. If you're working with a shoestring budget, skip the restaurant and offer a simple in-house buffet.

- Treat your most productive speakers to a special event—perhaps movie tickets, or a day's pass to a theme park. Allow them to bring along a spouse or friend to make up for all those times when their speaking assignments kept them away from home.

- Hire a motivational speaker to address the bureau at an annual gathering. This appearance by a professional speaker will not only serve as a reward but also will rev up the bureau's members for their own assignments.

A wide range of organizations from utilities to hospitals have asked me to speak at their recognition dinners. On these occasions, I want to make my speeches both informational and motivational, with a hefty dose of humor. My goal? To give the bureau members an enjoyable evening—and also inspire them to improve their own speeches.

- Ask the CEO to send your speakers bureau members a personal letter of appreciation. An added touch: frame the letter, so members can put it on display.

PERFORMANCE STANDARDS

There's no sense in giving speeches unless you know they're accomplishing something. If you provide your audiences with an evaluation form, you'll gain valuable information about the success (or failure) of your bureau's presentations.

Be sure to keep your evaluation forms simple. If you make them complex and time-consuming, no one will bother to fill them out—and you'll lose valuable insights into the effectiveness of your speakers bureau.

A simple evaluation form would include these basics:

- Speaker? excellent . . . good . . . fair . . . poor

- Content? useful . . . not relevant to my needs

- What did you like best about the program?

- Can you suggest any changes?

- What topics would you like to see in the future?

- Are you active in any other groups that might like to hear one of our free presentations? (If so, please give your name, phone number, and e-mail so we can contact you.)

LETTING THE COMMUNITY KNOW
ABOUT YOUR PROGRAMS

It doesn't do much good to have terrific speakers in your bureau if no one knows about them. So, make it a priority to publicize your bureau's programs.

Start by putting information on your company's Web site. Provide photographs of your speakers. (Good photos are mandatory. Anything that looks like a mug shot must be redone. Anything ten years old must be redone.) Make their credentials strong. Include blurbs from previous audiences.

Add a line about your speakers bureau to every single letter that goes out—a PS line would be the perfect place to add this info. Put a link to your speakers bureau in all email signatures. Note your speakers bureau on all business cards. Promote your programs on social media. Place listings in community calendars.

The possibilities are unlimited.

APPROPRIATE FORUMS

When you're just starting your speakers bureau, you'll welcome almost any audience—just to give your speakers something to do.

But as you receive more speaking invitations, you'll become increasingly choosy about your audiences. After all, you simply won't have enough time to accept every invitation that comes your way.

How to pick and choose the best forums for your purposes? Consider:

- *Size:* Will the audience be large enough to justify your expenditure of time, effort, and money?

- *Type of meeting:* Women's club luncheon? Professional panel meeting? Civic forum? Community event? Senior citizen social gathering? Ask yourself, "Will this meeting give us an *appropriate* forum to deliver our message?"

- *Typical speaker:* Ask: "Who spoke at last month's meeting? And the month before that?" You'll gain some insights into the type of programs they run—and the type of attention or inattention you can expect from this particular audience.

- *Agenda:* What other activities will be part of the program? Who else will be speaking, entertaining, fund-raising, recruiting, et cetera, at this event? For example, if you've been asked to talk to senior citizens about energy conservation, but the meeting's *main* event is a musical program . . . well, read the writing on the wall, decline the invitation, and direct your efforts to an audience where you'll get more attention and a better return on your speaking investment.

FIFTEEN

SPEECHWRITERS: HOW TO HIRE ONE AND HOW TO WORK WITH ONE

We can't all do everything.

—VIRGIL

When Gerald Ratner, the world's largest jewelry retailer, gave a speech at London's Albert Hall, he offered these four rules to becoming a multimillionaire:

1. Understand your market.
2. Form clear quality goals.
3. Evaluate your product against the competition's.
4. Don't write your own speeches.

There's truth in that last point!

The fact is: Very few senior executives have the *time* to write their own speeches. After all, it's simply not cost-effective for CEOs to spend weeks laboring over a speech when they should be doing what they're paid to do, which is *run a company.*

What's more, very few senior executives have the *inclination* to write their own speeches. They're businesspeople—not writers—so it's only natural for them to be more comfortable managing business details than putting pen to paper (or, finger to keyboard).

And, yes, let's be brutally honest: Very, *very* few senior executives have the *talent* to write their own speeches. After all, speech-writing is a highly demanding specialty . . . so specialized, in fact, that most professional writers don't do it well.

Why? Because the process of writing a speech is quite different from writing a memo, or a press release, or a quarterly report—and woe be to anyone who fails to grasp this vital difference.

Assume nothing. People might blog about speechwriting, but that doesn't make them a speechwriter. (Consider: Someone might edit a medical publication, but that doesn't make them a doctor.) Again, assume nothing. Ask questions. Check credentials—closely.

If *you* think you would benefit from hiring the expertise of a professional speechwriter (either on staff or as a freelance/consultant), start by asking other businesspeople for referrals. Then, use these practical questions to choose someone who's right *for you.*

- "How long have you been writing speeches?" If you need to give high-level speeches, then you need a speechwriter with experience. How much experience? Well, the more important your speech, the more savvy you need from your speechwriter. You want someone who has handled a great number of speech-writing assignments . . . someone who can anticipate problems and prevent problems . . . someone who can approach any speechwriting assignment with skill, confidence, and aplomb.

  On the other hand, every speechwriter has to start some-where. So, if you're willing to provide some supervision, why not hire a talented writer who's new to speechwriting? With some mentoring and professional training, you'll soon have an "experienced" speechwriter—and for much lower cost.

  I will forever remember the wonderful woman who gave me my first crack at speechwriting—advertising great Jane Maas. When she took me under her wing, I didn't have one bit of experience as a speechwriter. But I was a good writer. I had gumption. And (above all) I was willing to work nights and weekends to help the team. Speechwriting credits soon followed.

- "Is speechwriting your specialty?" This is a critical factor. If the writer is a generalist—that is, someone who does press releases one day, brochures the next, and speeches whenever they come along—you simply won't get the benefit of a well-tuned speechwriter's "ear."

Tip:
The location of your business need not limit you. Even if you operate out of a small town, you still have access to top speechwriting talent. A phone and e-mail will connect you with talented speechwriters around the country. So, don't limit yourself unnecessarily by imposing geographical restrictions.

- "Do you do all of the speechwriting yourself—or do you subcontract some assignments?"

  I cannot stress this point enough. Beware of any speechwriter or any public relations firm that takes a "group approach" to speechwriting.

  Case in point: Many PR firms will try to impress the client by sending high-ranking representatives to preliminary meetings, but then secretly "farm out" the actual speechwriting job to an unidentified freelancer. Quite often, to cut corners, PR firms choose the least-expensive freelancers they can get—and then the client (who paid top dollar to get a big-name PR firm) wonders why the submitted speech looks so amateurish.

  One other serious consideration: If a PR firm subcontracts its speeches to freelance writers you don't know, how can you be sure your material is being treated confidentially? How can you be sure the unseen and unscreened freelancers aren't also taking assignments from your competitors?

  Again, you're always better off developing a one-on-one relationship with a professional independent speechwriter you can trust implicitly.

- "Who are your current or recent clients?"

- "Do you have long-standing relationships with your clients? For example, how many speeches have you done for the XYZ Corporation?"

- "What do you know about the issues my industry faces?" Professional speechwriters prepare for interviews by reading about your company and your industry. Accept nothing less.

- "What's your educational background?"

  Caution: Don't think speechwriters need a particular degree in communications, public relations, or journalism. That's a misconception.

  What matters is a bright mind, a keen interest in the world, a knack for creative listening, an ability to learn new material quickly, a sensitivity about language, and a deep love for the spoken word. Period.

- "What's your professional background?" *Another caution:* Nobody really *begins* a career as a speechwriter. No twenty-two-year-old, fresh out of college and lacking real-life business experience, steps into a speechwriting slot and simply keeps moving up the speechwriting ladder, decade after decade. (And if they did . . . well, frankly, I'd be highly suspicious of their too-narrow background.) Speechwriting is often the culmination of several dynamic career interests.

- "Can you offer constructive criticism?" No head-nodders who will say anything to please the boss! You're looking for a bright individual who can tell you what you're doing wrong with your speeches—and show you how to improve.

- "Can you work quickly?"

  Here's an all-too-common scenario:

  Over two months ago, you asked your PR department to write an important speech, but they got tied up producing the annual report, or fielding media questions, or dealing with an employee crisis . . . whatever.

Anyhow, they waited until the last minute to write your speech, and now (not surprisingly) their draft looks like it was slapped together during a lunch hour.

You're dissatisfied. You're frustrated. You wanted a *terrific* speech for this important occasion, and now you're stuck—with only five days left.

It's times like these when you're glad you've already got a freelance speechwriter listed in your address book—someone you can call upon to work quickly and produce a quality manuscript. Treat this person like gold.

If you *don't* already know a speechwriter like this, resolve to start interviewing *now* so you'll never be caught unprepared again.

- "Would you provide recommendations from your clients?" Be specific. Ask for names and titles. For example, a beginning speechwriter might brag that he's worked for "many executives at Fortune 500 companies"—when, in fact, he did only one actual assignment involving a group of mid-level managers. Learn to probe for references and honest responses.

- "Would you show me some samples of your work?" *Warning:* Truly professional speechwriters do *not* pass out samples casually. They're discreet. They consider their speeches to be the property of their clients.

So, respect their professionalism and don't ask to see any confidential material.

A much better alternative: Speechwriters can provide *excerpts* of recent speeches, or they can individually ask their clients for permission to distribute a particular manuscript.

- "Would you do a line-edit during the interview?" Very simple: Give applicants a rough draft of a short-to-medium length speech (maybe 5–10 pages), and ask them to line-edit the speech. Give them no more than twenty to thirty minutes. You want to see how quickly they can work . . . how well they can spot errors . . . how gracefully they can rewrite an awkward line . . . how smoothly they can add rhetorical devices to create style.

  Tip: Make sure your speechwriting test has some basic errors in it: charts that don't add up to 100 percent, dates that are incorrect (i.e., Thursday, March 12, not Thursday, March 21), names that are misspelled, etc.

- "Do your speeches get media coverage?" Top speechwriters know how to write attention-getting speeches that prove irresistibly quotable to reporters. Their speeches are often quoted in *The New York Times,* or cited in significant trade publications, or noted by bloggers. These speechwriters can help you get valuable media attention for your company—attention that will enhance your professional status, promote your products, tout your services, build credibility for your organization, and draw attention to the issues of your industry. Not surprisingly, these speechwriters can command more money. They are well worth it.

- "Have you won any speechwriting awards?" Look for breadth of recognition. I'd rather hire a speechwriter whose three awards come from three different professional organizations, rather than all from the same group.

- "Would you be willing to look at three of my recent speeches and offer a critique?" Since you're asking a professional writer to do professional work, you need to offer payment. The fee can be a modest token, but as a business you need to offer.

Only a desperate nonprofessional would accept an assignment without pay. And you wouldn't want a desperate nonprofessional to come work on your team.

- "Would you accept a short speechwriting assignment so I can see the way we'd work together?" It doesn't have to be a big speech, the first time around. Just assign something short—say, an introduction, or a retirement tribute, or an award presentation. Something that will allow the two of you to work together as a team on an exploratory basis.

  Again, you will want to pay for this initial assignment—a modest token fee, but a fee, nonetheless.

- "Would you describe your fee structure?" You have a right to ask for cost estimates in advance. Your speechwriter may well offer you a price *range,* depending on how complex the assignment becomes.

  For example, if a speech requires two on-site meetings, it will cost more than if the same speech could be accomplished via phone and e-mail.

Remember:

To your speechwriter, time *is* money. The more efficient and streamlined the process, the lower the total fee. Consider also the deadline you're giving the speechwriter. The tighter the deadline, the greater the fee.

Experienced speechwriters are used to being brought in at the last minute, and they're used to working nights, weekends, and holidays to help clients beat a deadline. But, be aware: They *will* charge more for these rush assignments.

So, if you ask professional speechwriters to do some rush assignments over Thanksgiving weekend, they may well give up their holiday plans to accommodate you—but they'll charge accordingly.

And, come to think of it, you wouldn't have it any other way, would you?

APPENDIX

*Buying books would be a good thing if we also
could buy the time to read them in: but as a rule
the purchase of books is often mistaken for the
appropriation of their contents.*
                                    —ARTHUR SCHOPENHAUER

A SPECIAL SECTION OF
NOT-TO-BE-MISSED BOOKS

Whether you *write* speeches, *give* speeches, or *listen* to speeches,
these books will provide you with a greater appreciation of the way
we use language to communicate. Some are new, some are old—
disregard the publication dates because these books are truly timeless.

Ailes, Roger and Jon Kraushar. *You Are the Message.* New York, 1989.
    The definitive book on messages and the media. No one
    has written a better one.

Boettinger, Henry M. *Moving Mountains: or The Art of Letting Others
    See Things Your Way.* New York: Macmillan, 1969. There's a
    reason why this book has been selling for decades. See for
    yourself.

Hall, Edward T. *The Silent Language: An anthropologist reveals how we communicate by our manners and behavior.* New York: Doubleday, 1959. A classic.

Lamott, Anne. *Bird by Bird: Some Instructions on Writing and Life.* New York: Pantheon Books, 1994.

Linders, Robert H. *No Safe Route.* Bloomington, IN: iUniverse, 2013. Quite simply, the highest caliber sermons I have ever seen. Brilliant writing.

Lipman, Doug. *The Storytelling Coach.* Little Rock, Ak: August House Publishers, 1995.

Noonan, Peggy. *What I Saw at the Revolution.* New York: Random House, 1990.

Osborne, Alex. *Your Creative Power.* New York: Scribner's, 1948. Osborne was the "O" in the legendary BBDO advertising agency. He codified brainstorming.

Pinker, Steven. *The Language Instinct.* New York: Morrow, 1994.

Rodenburg, Patsy. *The Actor Speaks: Voice and the Performer.* New York: St. Martin's Press, 2000.

Roman, Kenneth and Jane Maas. *How to Advertise: A professional guide for the advertiser. What works. What doesn't. And why.* New York: St. Martin's Press, 1976. If you think of your speech as an advertisement, you will learn much from this small book.

Truss, Lynne. *Eats, Shoots & Leaves.* New York: Penguin, 2003. Who knew punctuation could be so fascinating?

Von Oech, Roger. *A Whack on the Side of the Head.* New York: Warner, 1990.

REFERENCE BOOKS

ANECDOTES

Bernard, Andre, and Clifton Fadiman. *The Bartlett's Book of Anecdotes,* revised edition. Boston, MA: Little, Brown, 2001. An updated version of the *Little, Brown Book of Anecdotes,* this book will always hold a prime spot on my bookshelf. It offers well-researched anecdotes about thousands of famous people through the ages, from Neil Armstrong and Bob Dole to Dorothy Parker and Xerxes. Valuable subject index, source list, and bibliography.

BIOGRAPHICAL QUOTATIONS

Ratcliffe, Susan, ed. *People on People: The Oxford Dictionary of Biographical Quotations*. New York, NY: Oxford University Press, 2001. Want to learn "who said what" about Margaret Thatcher, or Picasso, or anybody else for that matter? Start here. You'll get pithy quotes with solid documentation.

BUSINESS

Woods, John. *The Quotable Executive*. New York: McGraw-Hill, 2000. It contains excellent biographical identification.

CALENDAR OR DAILY LISTINGS

Dickson, Paul. *Timelines: Day by Day and Trend by Trend from the Dawn of the Atomic Age to the Gulf War*. Reading, MA: Addison Wesley Publishing, 1991. This is the best book of its kind. Suppose your organization was founded in 1971, and you want to find interesting details about that year. This book offers great tidbits that can make any presentation more interesting. In 1971, for example:

- The term "workaholic" worked itself into the language.
- The first handheld calculator was marketed for $249.
- Smiley-faced buttons popped up everywhere.

COMMENCEMENTS

Ross, Alan, ed. *Speaking of Graduation*. Nashville, TN: Walnut Grove Press, 2001. Excerpts from graduation speeches—both serious and humorous.

DEFINITIONS

Brussell, Eugene E. *Webster's New World Dictionary of Quotable Definitions.* Englewood Cliffs, NJ: Prentice-Hall, 1988. Disregard the old publication date. This book is worth its weight in gold for any speaker. Need a clever definition? Forget your regular dictionary. Instead, turn to this book for more than 17,000 lively definitions on 2,000 subjects.

- *Exercise:* "A modern superstition, invented by people who ate too much and had nothing to think about." (George Santayana)

- *Inflation:* "Too much money going to somebody else." (William Vaughan)

- *San Francisco:* "A city of four seasons every day." (Bob Hope)

DESIGN, CHARTS, AND TYPOGRAPHY

Duarte, Nancy. *Resonate: Present Visual Stories that Transform Audiences.* New York: Wiley, 2010. Nancy Duarte's visual work is in a class of its own.

Tufte, Edward R. *Envisioning Information.* Cheshire, CT: Graphics Press LLC, 13th printing, 2011. If you want to learn about the visual display of statistical information, you turn to Tufte.

Tufte, Edward R., *Visual Explanations: Images and Quantities, Evidence and Narrative.* Cheshire, CT: Graphics Press LLC, 9th printing 2010.

Zelazny, Gene. *Say It With Charts: The Executive's Guide to Successful Presentations.* Homewood, IL: Dow Jones-Irwin, 1985. Again, ignore the publication date of this book. It's a classic. It's not bound by the fashion whims of any day. This author provides timeless advice for anyone who ever has to use charts in presentations—which is to say, most of the speaking world.

Zelazny was Director of Visual Communications for McKinsey & Company, Inc. That credential speaks for itself. Before you start putting pie charts in front of audiences, take this man's advice.

ENTERTAINMENT

Rees, Nigel. *Cassell's Movie Quotations*. London: Cassell, 2000. Great lines from the movies, from moviemakers, and from movie fans. Outstanding resource.

EULOGIES

McNees, Pat, ed. *Dying: A Book of Comfort*. New York: Warner Books, 1998. A diverse collection of quotations, prayers, and literary passages about the subject of death. McNees provides excellent cross-cultural material covering a wide range of situations:

- the death of a child
- the death of a parent
- the death of a spouse
- long good-byes
- sudden deaths
- suicides

This is a valuable resource for anyone of any faith who must deliver a eulogy.

HISTORY

Axelrod, Alan. *The Quotable Historian*. New York: McGraw-Hill, 2000. It contains dozens of thematic sections.

POLITICS, GOVERNMENT, AND MILITARY

Torricelli, U.S. senator Robert. *Quotations for Public Speakers*. New Brunswick, NJ: Rutgers University Press, 2001. This is a historical, literary, and political anthology—with topics ranging from diplomacy to justice to urban affairs.

William B. Whitman, ed. *The Quotable Politician*. Connecticut: The Lyons Press, 2003.

- "You won't find average Americans on the left or on the right. You'll find them at Kmart." (Zell Miller)

- "You must do the thing you think you cannot do." (Eleanor Roosevelt)

- "In politics, if you want anything said, ask a man; if you want anything done, ask a woman." (Margaret Thatcher)

- "If there is one basic element in our Constitution, it is civilian control of the military." (Harry S. Truman)

PREDICTIONS

Lee, Laura. *Bad Predictions: 2000 Years of the Best Minds Making the Worst Forecasts.* Rochester, MI: Elsewhere Press, 2000.

PUBLIC SPEAKING

Carter, Judy. *The Message of You.* New York: St. Martin's Press, 2013. If you want to become a paid professional speaker, then you need to read this book. This author knows what she's talking about.

Detz, Joan. *It's Not What You Say, It's How You Say It.* New York: St. Martin's Press, 2002. Get help with voice, body language, eye contact, audio-visual, ad-libs, etc. Make your speaking style reinforce your message.

Hoff, Ron. *I Can See You Naked.* Kansas City, MI: Andrews McMeel, 1992. Fine information for anyone who has to give a presentation.

QUOTATIONS–GENERAL

Bowden, Paul. *Smart Quotations for Smart People.* Kindle edition, 2011.

Frank, Leonard Roy. *Quotionary.* New York: Random House, 2001. This is a huge collection—particularly strong in contemporary sources.

- *Longevity:* "I attribute it to red meat and gin." (Julia Child)

Swainson, Bill, ed. *Encarta Book of Quotations*. New York: St. Martin's Press, 2000. An outstanding reference work with more than 25,000 quotations, plus context notes giving additional background information. You'll find a strong emphasis on international figures from the last one hundred years.

RELIGION AND PHILOSOPHY

Peck, M. Scott, M.D. *Abounding Grace*. Kansas City, MI: Andrews McMeel, 2000. An inspirational collection of quotations about happiness, courage, compassion, purity, perseverance, courtesy, faith, goodness, love, respect, strength, and wisdom.

Tomlinson, Gerald. *Treasury of Religious Quotations*. Englewood Cliffs, NJ: Prentice-Hall, 1991. Subdivided into thirty religions and beliefs (with otherwise hard-to-find entries from Mormonism and Taoism).

SCIENCE

Fripp, Jon, Michael Fripp, and Deborah Fripp. *Speaking of Science: Notable Quotes on Science, Engineering, and the Environment*. Eagle Rock, VA: LLH Technology Publishing, 2000. It's an essential reference.

SPORTS

Tomlinson, Gerald, ed. *Speaker's Treasury of Sports Anecdotes, Stories, and Humor*. Englewood Cliffs, NJ: Prentice-Hall, 1990. Quotes from fifty-four different sports and activities. Note: It also offers a sports calendar and birthday listings for famous athletes (both are useful resources for "this date in history" material).

STATISTICS

Gaither, C. C, and A. E. Cavozov-Gaither. *Statistically Speaking*. Philadelphia, PA: Institute of Physics Publishing, 1996. Again, disregard the old publication date. This remains the most comprehensive collection of quotations pertaining to statistics, with detailed bibliography and indices. It has a surprisingly wide range of chapters, including:

- *Data:* "It is a capital mistake to theorize before one has the data." (Sherlock Holmes, a character created by Arthur Conan Doyle)

- *Graphics:* "You can draw a lot of curves through three graph points. You can extrapolate it a lot of ways." (Michael Crichton)

- *Statistician:* "Most of you would as soon be told that you are cross-eyed or knock-kneed as that you are destined to be a statistician." (Josiah Stamp)

TOASTS, ROASTS, AND SPECIAL OCCASIONS

Detz, Joan. *Can You Say a Few Words?* New York: St. Martin's Press, 2006.

Each chapter presents practical speaking advice for special occasions, including:

- award ceremonies

- retirements

- sports banquets

- patriotic ceremonies

- anniversary tributes

- commencements

- eulogies

Dickson, Paul. *Toasts: Over 1500 of the Best Toasts, Sentiments, Blessings and Graces.* New York: Bloomsbury USA, 2009. No professional speechwriter will want to work without this book handy. It's wonderful.

Evans, William R., and Andrew Frothingham. *Well-Done Roasts.* New York: St. Martin's Press, 1992. Zingers from many sources and for many occasions:

- *Retirement:* "We're not sure what we'll do without him . . . but we've been thinking about it for years."

- "As Walter Kerr (*New York Times* theater critic) said, 'He has delusions of adequacy.'"

- "So, you're going to try and roast me. Well, in the words of that Pat Benatar song, 'Hit me with your best shot, fire away.'"

- "As Sir Walter Walker said, 'Britain has invented a new missile. It's called the civil servant—it doesn't work and it can't be fired.'"

Irwin, Dale. *The Everything Toasts Book.* Holbrook, MA: Adams Media, 2000. A toast for every special occasion.

WEB SITES FOR SPEAKERS

AMERICAN INDIAN TALES

www.kstrom.net/isk/stories/myths.html

APHORISMS, PROVERBS, AND QUOTATIONS

www.altiusdirectory.com/Society/hat-quotes.php (Special occasion quotes, from Santa Claus to All Saints Day)

www.aphorismsgalore.com (Wide-ranging categories: art and literature, science and religion, work and recreation, etc)

www.brainyquote.com/quotes/keywords/speeches.html

www.columbia.edu/acis/bartleby/bartlett (Outstanding reference sources: *Bartlett's Familiar Quotations, Simpson's Contemporary Quotations,* and many more)

www.creativequotations.com (Proverbs from more than 300 countries and cultures.)

www.famous-quotations.com (Searchable by category, author, and
   country)

www.navy.mil/navydata/leadership/mist.asp?x=S

www.presentationmagazine.com/presentation-quotes-and-quota
   tions-7498.htm

ARTS AND LETTERS

www.aldaily.com/

BIOGRAPHICAL INFORMATION

www.s9.com (You can search this biographical dictionary by birth
   years, death years, titles, professions, literary or artistic
   works, and key achievements.)

DATES IN HISTORY

www.infoplease.com

JOURNALISM AND PUBLISHING

www.cjr.org/ (From *Columbia Journalism Review,* interesting perspectives on speeches, including how journalists cover speeches.)

www.cjr.org/www.editorandpublisher.com (Perspectives on speeches
   from the media.)

www.publetariart.com (Information on getting published.)

www.publishersweekly.com/pw/home/index/htm. (Ideas and insights
   for speakers who might want to develop their speeches into
   a book.)

MYTHS AND LEGENDS

www.mythiccrossroads.com/site_map.htm (Aesop's fables; Arthu-
   rian legends; Norse, Greek, and Egyptian gods and god-
   desses; African tales; and a particularly good section on
   characters of the Wild West.)

SOCIAL MEDIA

http://socialmediatoday.com/

www.foliomag.com/

SPEECH TEXTS

www.af.mil/information/speeches/index.asp (Transcripts of U.S. Air Force speeches)

www.army.mil/info/institution/speeches/ (Transcripts of U.S. Army speeches)

http://gos.sbc.edu/top100.html ("Top 100 speeches of the 20th century." Supported by Sweet Briar College. Includes interesting speeches by prominent women.)

www.hillsdale.edunews/imprimis.asp (Wide range of speeches covering cultural, economic, political, and educational issues.)

www.historychannel.com (Speeches by business, political, and academic leaders.)

www.historyplace.com/speeches (You'll find a wide assortment of speech texts, from St. Francis of Assisi's "Sermon to the Birds" to Lou Gehrig's "Farewell to Yankee Fans," to Bill Clinton's "I Have Sinned.")

www.navy.mil/navydata/leadership/mist.asp?x=S (Transcripts of U.S. Navy speeches)

www.raf.mod.uk/history/airpowerspeechesarchived.cfm (Transcripts of British Royal Air Force speeches)

www.uscg.mil/seniorleadership/speeches.asp (Transcripts of U.S. Coast Guard speeches)

www.winstonchurchill.org (Speeches, quotations, and anecdotes of Winston Churchill.)

STATISTICS

www.guardian.co.uk/data

U.S. HISTORY

www.law.ou.edu/hist/ (University of Oklahoma's College of Law. Historical speeches and political documents, from the pre-Colonial era to the present.)

ORGANIZATIONS: RESOURCES FOR
BOTH SPEAKERS AND SPEECHWRITERS

American Communication Association: www.americancomm.org

American Library Association: www.ala.org

American Medical Writers Association: www.amwa.org/default .asp?Mode=DirectoryDisplay&id=1&DirectoryUseAbsolu teOnSearch=True

American Professional Speakers Association: http://speakersassocia tion.org/AmericanProfessionalSpeakersAssociation.html

American Society of Journalists and Authors: www.asja.org

American Statistical Association: www.amstat.org

Asian American Journalists Association: www.aaja.org/

Association for Women in Communications: www.womcom.org

Association of Professional Communication Consultants: http:// consultingsuccess.org/wp

Construction Writers Association: www.constructionwriters.org/

Editorial Freelancers Association: www.the-efa.org/

International Association of Business Communicators: www.iabc .com

Military Writers Society of America: www.mwsadispatches.com/

National Association of Government Communicators: www.nagc .com

National Association of Independent Writers and Editors: http:// naiwe.com/

National Association of Science Writers: www.nasw.org

National Black Public Relations Society: www.nbprs.org

National Communication Association: www.natcom.org

National Education Writers Association: www.ewa.org

National Rural Electric Cooperatives Association: www.nreca.org

National Speakers Association: www.nsaspeaker.org

National Storytelling Network: www.storynet.org

National Writers Association: www.nationalwriters.com/page/page
/1963103.htm

Native American Journalists Association: www.naja.com/

NY Women in Communications: www.nywici.org

PEN (International Association of Poets, Playwrights, Editors,
Essayists, and Novelists): www.pen.org

Poetry Society of America: www.poetrysociety.org/psa/

Professional Speakers Guild: www.professionalspeakersguild.com

Public Relations Society of America: www.prsa.org

Publicity Club of New York: www.publicityclub.org

Society of Environmental Journalists: www.sej.org

Toastmasters International: www.toastmasters.org. Toastmasters deserves a special note—and not just because it's big (this
nonprofit organization has more than 275,000 members).
Toastmasters deserves special attention because it has helped
so many people become better speakers and better leaders.
No matter where you live, there's a Toastmasters where you
can develop your potential.

FOR SPEAKERS REQUESTING
SPECIAL VOICE HELP:

American Speech-Language-Hearing Association: www.asha.org

Australian Speak Easy Association: www.speakeasy.org.au

British Stammering Association: www.stammering.org

Canadian Stuttering Association: www.stutter.ca

International Stuttering Association: www.isastutter.org

National Stuttering Association: www.westutter.org

Stuttering Foundation: www.stutteringhelp.org

INDEX